DATE DUE			
Oct 8 '75			
Oct 29 '75			
Nov 3 '82			

The Poetry of Greek Tragedy

THE POETRY OF GREEK TRAGEDY

by *Richmond Lattimore*

THE JOHNS HOPKINS PRESS

Baltimore

Standard Book Number 8018-0364-0

Originally published, 1958
Second printing, 1965
Third printing, 1969

Foreword

THESE six lectures were given at The Johns Hopkins University in January, 1957, on the Percy Turnbull Memorial Lectureship of Poetry. They are here printed without substantial alteration. The notes and bibliography are not supposed to represent an adequate guide to the critical literature on an enormous subject, but are rather intended as an acknowledgment of principal works consulted in preparing these limited studies.[1]

The translations in the text are all my own. The University of Chicago Press holds the copyright for the translations from Euripides, *Alcestis* and *Helen*.

I wish here to express my thanks to the donors of The Percy Turnbull Memorial Lectureship and to The Johns Hopkins Press for making this book possible, and to the academic community of The Johns Hopkins University for abundant generosity and kindness at the time of the lectures.

[1] The rather few references to critical works in the notes are given in the simplest possible form. Bibliographical information on these works will be found in the bibliography at the end of the book.

Contents

FOREWORD, PAGE V

INTRODUCTION, PAGE 3

CHAPTER I, PAGE 11
Aeschylus, *The Suppliant Maidens*

CHAPTER II, PAGE 28
Aeschylus, *The Persians*
The Seven against Thebes
Prometheus Bound

CHAPTER III, PAGE 56
Sophocles, *Ajax*

CHAPTER IV, PAGE 81
Sophocles, *Oedipus Tyrannus*

CHAPTER V, PAGE 103
Euripides, *Medea*
Helen

CHAPTER VI, PAGE 126
Euripides, *The Bacchae*

CONCLUSION, PAGE 146

BIBLIOGRAPHY, PAGE 149

INDEX OF PASSAGES, PAGE 151

The Poetry of Greek Tragedy

Introduction

W H A T is an Attic tragedy? Its essential nature must be defined by those features which qualified a play for presentation in the formal competition for a prize at the city Dionysia (perhaps in other public, religious competitions as well).[1] If we knew the origin and early history of this form, we should have to take it into account. But we do not.[2] We have to enter from the other end, and work from the common elements which are found in the corpus of extant tragedy: thirty-two complete tragedies, plus a large number of fragments and résumés.

As for quality, a tragedy was required to be dignified and serious. The principal purpose was to enact a heroic story, drawn from legend. There were few exceptions. The plays

[1] After writing the first pages of these studies, I came across the following statement (read ten years earlier and since half forgotten) of Wilamowitz, Introduction to Euripides: *Herakles*, p. 107: "Wir stehen am schlusse: es ist nur noch nötig, den ertrag unserer betrachtungen zusammenzuziehen, damit die frage beantwortet werde, was ist eine attische tragödie? eine attische tragödie ist ein in sich abgeschlossenes stück der heldensage, poetisch bearbeitet in erhabenen stile für die darstellung durch einen attischen bürgerchor und zwei bis drei schauspieler, und bestimmt als teil des öffentlichen gottesdienstes im heiligtume des Dionysos aufgeführt zu werden." For the circumstances and rules governing competitive performance, see Pickard-Cambridge, *The Dramatic Festivals of Athens*.

[2] Consider, for example, the remark of Aristotle *Poetics* 4.1449ᴀ: "Tragedy began as improvisation . . . by those who led off the dithyramb." I cannot dispute this, nor can I make the slightest use of it in trying to understand the tragedy (or dithyramb) which has come down to us. I do not mean to question the value of studies in the origin of tragedy.

were presented impersonally: that is, even when present day stories were used, present day public characters could not be named; nor could the poet speak in his own person.

A tragedy, as entrant for competition, had to be so constructed as not to require more than a stated allowance of players, that is, actors, supernumeraries, and chorus. It had to be written in verse, not prose, and had to use language which was not always the language of prose.[3] The verse was unrhymed but, whether it was blank verse or stanzaic (spoken or sung), it obeyed canons more strict than any which have ever been observed in (for instance) English verse.

From these bare essentials, other common features of tragedy follow. The requirement that a tragedy be serious and dignified allows wit, but precludes horseplay; the same requirement perhaps accounts for the tragic poet's habit of reporting violent action rather than staging it;[4] and for the avoidance of certain metrical forms which were used in comedy.[5] It is important to remember that dignity and

---

[3] Take as an instance Aeschylus' *The Suppliant Maidens* 93–95:

δαυλοὶ γὰρ πραπίδων
δάσκιοί τε τείνουσιν πόροι
κατιδεῖν ἄφραστοι.

These lines belong characteristically to tragedy, not only in virtue of the ideas, imagery, and meter, but also in the use of the words δαυλός, πράπιδες, and δασκιός, and in the arrangement of δαυλοί and ἄφραστοι in relation to the subject and main verb of the sentence.

[4] Horseplay, including slapstick pursuits, fisticuffs, etc., seems to be required in Attic Old Comedy, a form which, despite its apparent looseness, has far more readily discernible "required elements" than tragedy.

[5] Comedy uses anapaestic tetrameter catalectic frequently, iambic tetrameter catalectic occasionally; tragedy does not use these at all, so far as I have found, for Aeschylus frg. 87 and Sophocles frg. 804 (Nauck) are both Aristophanic lines and may very well have been adapted by the comic poet to his own meters. There are many other differences, and dignity is probably not the only consideration. It is worth noting that

seriousness do not require that a tragedy be "tragical" in the modern sense that it must be the story of a disaster. Whether or not the play has a happy ending depends principally on the way the legend (or myth) ends. The story of Oedipus demands an unhappy ending: the story of Philoctetes, which is an equally popular legend for tragedy, demands a happy ending. We are justified in using such terms as "romantic comedy" which are helpful toward definition by modern standards, but we ought to remember that, technically speaking, *Iphigenia in Tauris* and *Helen* are tragedies, just as certainly as *Medea* and *The Trojan Women* are. Otherwise, the danger is that we shall form a set of tragic standards based on a few plays, and then try to torture the other plays into conforming to those standards.

Now, if a play, in order to be called tragedy, does not necessarily have to tell the story of extreme suffering or disaster, it will follow *a fortiori* (or so I think) that those moral or spiritual narrative concepts which, so to speak, justify suffering and disaster—such as pride and punishment, tragic fault, learning through suffering—are not part of the essential definition of tragedy. This does not mean that we are wrong to interpret in these terms, when the terms work. Sometimes, but not always, the poets themselves seem to use such concepts. Again, the serious tone and the solemn occasion do, in fact, dictate moralizing (though not any one particular group of morals); and the implicit or explicit use of divinity and religion (though not of any particular gods or any particular rituals).

What we can put down, then, as the essential *facts* of tragedy are:

iambic tetrameter catalectic is the standard verse for folk ballads and heroic poetry in Modern Greek.

The presentation under strict competitive rules on a public occasion which, like all public occasions in Athens, was under religious sanction.

Dignity and seriousness and objectivity (as contrasted with comedy and satyr-play).

Contingent upon these: the raising of moral and religious issues.

The primary purpose, to enact a story from Greek legend.

The facts of poetry.

The critics of Greek tragedy have, however, disagreed over what is essential, what is secondary and derivative, and likewise what is important or interesting.[6] Some have held that tragedy began as a sacred, ceremonial story and remained essentially that, even where it appears most secular and heroic.[7] Others have emphasized the moral and theological aspects, and have seen the tragic poet as a prophet with a vocation who through drama tried to interpret the gods to his people and teach them the way of right action.[8] Others again have read the tragedies as purely dramatic constructions,[9] emphasizing plot, motivation, or character, according to the critic's main interest. In addition to these

[6] See, in general, Schmid, *Geschichte der griechischen Literatur*, II, 27–50, and especially p. 29, with bibliography to date.

[7] The best known form of this type of interpretation is perhaps that stated by Murray, "Excursus on the Ritual Forms Preserved in Greek Tragedy," incorporated in Harrison, *Themis*, pp. 340–63; restated and defended, *Encyclopaedia Britannica*, s.v. "Drama."

[8] See, above all, Pohlenz, *Die griechische Tragödie*, p. 31. The calling of the tragic poet involved "das Recht und die Verantwortung dafür, Lehrer seines Volkes zu sein." The view is consistently maintained. A similar position, differently developed, is maintained by Jaeger, *Paideia* I, pp. 237–85, 332–81.

[9] This is the approach of, for instance, Kitto, *Greek Tragedy*; Waldock, *Sophocles the Dramatist*; T.v. Wilamowitz, *Die dramatische Technik des Sophokles*.

general views, there have been many special technical studies of particular aspects: indispensable works on the anatomy of verse, for example, proceeding through analysis and statistics, treating the meters of Greek tragedy scientifically without more than secondary regard to the nature of the plays as a whole. Apart from such studies, however, I have found relatively little interest in the poetry of Greek tragedy. What I have said of the moralizing approach seems equally true of the literary approach: most critics might most of the time be discussing plays which were written in plain prose.

I do not here wish to reverse the trend of criticism, nor to question, except incidentally, the validity of approaches other than mine. Is Sophocles the artificer of lines, the master of sound combinations, the painter of images and architect of rhetorical figures, more important, more basic, more the true Sophocles, than Sophocles the moralist, Sophocles the student of character, or Sophocles the storyteller? I may have my notions, but I do not mean to argue them. I suspect myself of creating a separation of aspects which are not entirely separable. But I wish to show, if I can, some of the ways in which the poetry as poetry contributes to the effect of the drama as drama—realizing that if the drama is written as poetry, not merely in verse, the distinction between the poetry as poetry and the drama as drama may sometimes be artificial and strained, sometimes even false.

I realize also that what I want to do is difficult and perhaps impossible, since I shall have to use translations which, though made to order for such use, will be inadequate, and since I cannot thrust my victim's head into the Greek text. Using translations, however, I shall try to do some such brutal thing, though I stand in the shadow of Basil Lanneau Gildersleeve, who himself had a weakness for verse translation but could never have dreamed of confusing it with scholarship. It is not easy at this point even to define what I mean by poetry, aside from the obvious facts of metrical and rhetorical structure, imagery, the use of words and forms not used in prose—subjects which can scarcely be dealt with except in a technical study. It is only easy to illustrate, piecemeal. Before I do this, I shall suggest some tentative and imperfect working formulas. One might investigate, for instance, the implications of this axiom: when you have outlined the plot, analyzed character and motive, articulated the moral issues—the residue is the poetry. This would be more nearly true if it were possible for all tragedies to be summarized without taking the poetry into consideration. We would not so account for the fact, if fact it is, that Euripides' *The Children of Heracles* contains very little poetry and his *Hippolytus* contains very little else. Or shall we say that what is directed neither to the emotion nor the intellect, but to the imagination, is the poetry of the plays? This is better: plays do not merely enact and instruct; they make us see what is not there. But imagination does not exhaust the content of the poetical either.

Nor are the three tragic poets alike. I suggest that we look for the special contribution of the poetry in some such phenomena as these: for Aeschylus, in enlargement; for Sophocles, in anomaly; for Euripides, in relief or idealization. For Aeschylus, poetry is basic—it comes first: this blows the simple plot and limited characterization into full scale drama. For Sophocles, drama comes first: in what puzzles or disturbs the coherent interpretation of complete drama, or at least stands unaccounted for in the economy, we may look for the poetry. For Euripides, sometimes at least, the point comes first. We may find his poetry in what seems to have nothing to do with the drama or in what is merely contrasted to it, or we may find his poetry, after all, in certain ideas or themes, succinctly expressed only in lyric terms, which yet hold all the meaning of the dramatic action. I hope these propositions are at least suggestive; I know that they are far too general to be of any use unless carried into particulars.

Before I proceed to such particulars, let me say as clearly as I can what my purpose in these studies will be. I am not trying to make a new definition of tragedy, nor to prove that the most important or interesting aspect of a given play is one aspect rather than another. I am not, principally, trying to prove anything. I am trying only to suggest ways of enlarging, and further vitalizing, our appreciation of what we are given.

I

AESCHYLUS

The Supplicant Maidens

The Suppliant Maidens

⌐⌐⌐⌐⌐⌐⌐⌐⌐⌐⌐⌐⌐⌐⌐⌐⌐⌐⌐⌐⌐⌐⌐⌐⌐

I WILL begin with the play which, though it
can no longer be thought of as the earliest extant tragedy,
yet stands closest to the form of dramatic lyric out of
which tragedy may have been shaped. This is *The Suppliant Maidens* of Aeschylus.[1] Io, daughter of Inachus and

---

[1] The trilogy plus satyr-play probably consists of *The Suppliant Maidens,
The Egyptians* or *The Builders* (Θαλαμόποιοι), *The Danaids* and *Amymone.* Despite two attractive fragments of *The Danaids,* one of which
seems to show that Aphrodite herself spoke in the play, we know very
little about the second two tragedies. See Smyth on frgs. 24 and 25 (frgs.
43 and 44, Nauck). Scholars in the past have almost unanimously assumed
that *The Suppliant Maidens* was the earliest extant tragedy, with tentative
dates ranging from 500 to 480 B.C. Such dates have been based on the
"primitive" characteristics of the play: the simplicity of the dramatic
action, the predominance of the Chorus, the thinly characterized acting
parts, etc. A recently discovered papyrus, however, testifies that a group of
Aeschylean plays which includes *The Danaids* and *Amymone* was successful
against Sophocles; see E. Lobel, E. P. Wegener, C. H. Roberts, *The
Oxyrynchus Papyri* (London, 1952), XX, no. 2256, frg. 3, pp. 30–31, with
the remarks of E. Lobel, who suggests that "a *terminus post quem* of 470

11

princess of Argos, was loved by Zeus and hated by Hera. Transformed into a cow and harried by the stinging fly which was the ghost of the herdsman Argos, she fled across the world to Egypt. There Zeus stroked her with his hand, and she conceived and bore a son, Epaphus (meaning "born of the touch"). From him, three generations later, were descended Danaus and Aegyptus. The fifty sons of Aegyptus desired to marry the fifty daughters of Danaus. These refused them and with their father fled across the sea, pursued by their suitors, to Argos. Here they took up a position as suppliants to the gods and the soil of Argos, their ancestral home, and threw themselves on the mercy of the Argive King, Pelasgus. He took responsibility for them and drove away the herald of the Egyptians who tried to pull them off by force. But subsequently the fifty girls were, after all, constrained to marry the fifty sons of Aegyptus. All but one murdered their husbands: Hypermestra alone, magnificently mendacious, spared hers, Lynceus.

Such is the legend followed by Aeschylus in a trilogy of which only the first play, *The Suppliant Maidens,* has come down to us. The tragedy begins with the entrance of the Danaids and closes with their departure to Argos after the repulse of the Egyptian Herald. The ancestral legend of Io and Egypt is presented through choral utterance and dialogue; the end of the myth, the sequels to *The Suppliant*

B.C. will hardly err by being too late." It might be well to consider once again whether *The Suppliant Maidens* is really more primitive than *The Persians* (472 B.C.) or *The Seven against Thebes* (467 B.C.), or, if it is, whether its character might not be dictated by the nature of the story. Mr. Lobel rightly reminds us that date of composition and date of performance are not necessarily the same thing; but to postulate that Aeschylus put this one on ice for years and then brought it out seems to me to be a desperate means of defense for a position which may not be worth defending.

Maidens, must be picked up and pieced out from a very few fragments and from later references and compilations.[2] The action of our tragedy, then, consists only in the arrival and self-introduction of the Chorus of Danaids, their persuasion of a somewhat reluctant Pelasgus to refer their cause to the Argive assembly and accept its vote to defend them by force, the attempt of the Egyptian Herald to drag them off and his repulse by Pelasgus at the head of an army, and their ultimate departure to safety in Argos—safety which is only provisional, for the Egyptian fleet is there, battle impends, the result is doubtful.

How does this simple series of simple events constitute a dramatic action? Where are the problems, issues, conflicts? The suppliant situation here is basic, and, drawn as it is from legend but reflecting as it does the problems of contemporary statecraft, it is to be one of the repeated story patterns of Attic tragedy.[3] Suppliants face the king of tragedy with a true dilemma. If he rejects them, he offends the gods; if he accepts them, he involves his state in war. But in the end, he must accept them, especially when, as in this play, they blackmail him with the threat of suicide —threatening to hang themselves in the sight of the gods of sanctuary. This time the poor King is a reluctant rescuer,

---

[2] Fragments under the appropriate titles in Smyth and Nauck; see above, note 1.

[3] In extant drama, we find Aeschylus' *The Suppliant Maidens;* Euripides' *The Children of Heracles* and *The Suppliant Women;* Sophocles' *Oedipus at Colonus.* There are interesting variants on the story pattern. In the first three, the "suppliant" is a group, in *The Children of Heracles,* even a group of supernumeraries without lines. Spokesmen in the Euripides plays are, respectively, Iolaus plus Macaria, and Aethra plus Adrastus. Aeschylus' group are their own spokesmen. Sophocles, as usual the most individual of the three, makes the "suppliant" an individual, Oedipus, merely assisted by his daughters; the protection of the suppliant is personal, not public, and carried through by Theseus without the questions of state policy elsewhere involved; the hateful Creon replaces the hateful herald.

almost comic in his distress. It is the helpless maidens who
have force of character. They overshadow also their father,
Danaus, who hovers about uneasily, offering sage counsel
but taking little part in the essential argument. Even such
character as he does show may not appropriately motivate
the sequel; the dear old gentleman with his counsels of
prudence will be the murderous father-in-law who commands his daughters to stab their bridegrooms.

We have, then, for action, suppliant posture, doubt and
defense, as we have seen; then both King and father are
withdrawn from the scene with naïve care, so that the girls
can be left alone, protected only by sanctuary from the
Herald of the Egyptians, who does not respect sanctuary
guaranteed by foreign gods. There follows a vivid scene
where the maidens, shouting almost incomprehensible in-
sults and answered in kind, are being haled away. How far
this was acted out in terms of physical struggle, how far
merely pantomimed and declaimed, we can only guess.
Then the King enters in the nick of time, the Herald is
chased away, though not for long; this will be only the prel-
ude to battle. The battle will come in the next play, and, of
course, it will not be enacted on stage.

In addition to actors and chorus, the allowance of supernumeraries seems lavish. The Danaids either have from the
start or acquire during the drama a handmaiden apiece;
Pelasgus enters attended on each occasion; Danaus con-
sciously indicates the guard of honor Argos has given him.
Yet the drama in its own way enacts far more than these
simple effects and themes. It is, for instance, an enactment
of basic oppositions, male against female, Greek against
barbarian, democracy against monarchy. It is about the sons
of Aegyptus, who never appear, and their past rejected court-
ship; and about Zeus in several aspects, unseen, and not
perfectly understood, and about Zeus and Io, the cow and

the fly far in the past. And all this is enacted in the poetry.

First, consider the simple enlargement of presented data. Danaus stage-directs the entrance of Pelasgus thus (180–83):

> I see dust, the silent messenger of armament,
> but there's no silence in the axles that are turning
> in the wheels. I see the army, the sloped shields
> and shaken spears, the horses and curved chariots.

Pelasgus will appear with at most one chariot, and perhaps two to a half-dozen men; but Danaus makes the audience see an army. The arrival of the fleet, which cannot, of course, be represented even symbolically on stage, is reported in more detail (713–23):

> From my watchpoint, sanctuary to suppliants, I see
> their craft, for it is well in sight, no detail lost.
> I recognize the trim of the sail, the side bulwarks,
> the prow with eyes tracing ahead the vessel's course,
> the steering oar rigged at the stern, by which she handles
> only too well, or so the ship's enemies think.
> Her seamen are seen plainly too, their swarthy limbs
> conspicuous in contrast to the white attire.
> The rest of their vessels and the whole supporting fleet
> show clearly also, but the flagship, close inshore,
> has furled her sail and rows in, with full power of oars.

With Danaus, the audience visualizes beyond the meager acting ground. When Pelasgus does appear, declaring his lineage, he projects, not without perplexity for philologists, a piece of that map of the world which Aeschylus seems to have carried in his mind (250–59):

> I am Pelasgus, son of Palaechthon the earth born,
> and I am commander of this nation.
> And after me, their king, a people rightly called

Pelasgian cultivate the country you behold.
And all the continent from the point where Strymon runs
his bright course, all to westward of him I control.
I claim within my confines the Perrhaebian land,
the further side of Pindus, near the Paeonians,
and the mountains of Dodona. The water of the sea cuts short
my kingdom westward. All from there to here, I rule.

Or what we see in front of us can also build pictures for
the imagination. Pelasgus, seeing the suppliants, naturally
asks who they are (234–36):

Whence comes this company? What is this unGreek array
in robes outlandish and the luxury
of close weft? How shall we hail you?

They answer, ultimately, that they are Argives; the King is
astounded, and here are the terms of his astonishment
(277–89):

O stranger maidens, it is hard for me to believe
you when you say that you are born of Argive blood.
For you are more like ladies of Africa
from the show of you, not like the women of our land.
Then too, the Cyprian look that's carved in female forms
by male artificers is your look. They say, again,
that nomad women, much as you are, sit astride
their saddled camels and ride them as if they were horses.
These live in the country next the Ethiopians.

This map-catalogue may be a display of garbled erudition
and padding in the play, but it is something more as well.
The suppliant situation is not to be disentangled from what
might be called the theme of the flight of the desirable
quarry, and the barbarous beauty of the suppliants is a part
of this. So their almost intolerable attractions are dwelt
on, even after the action of the play is done, in Danaus'
last advices (994–1005):

The resident alien finds every tongue is quick to speak
evil of him. The slander that clings is easily said.
I would warn you, then, against what might destroy my name.
You have the time of youth on you that turns men's eyes.
Such luscious ripening is not easy to guard.
Wild beasts ravage it, so do men. Why not? There are
fierce creatures that fly the air and things that walk the ground.
And Aphrodite calls attention to the fruit
grown ripe within the orchard when the door is forced.[4]
And the shape and glory of maiden figures work to make
all those who pass try the enchantment of their eyes
in flights of arrows, overmastered by desire.

The girls are fleeing from marriage. *That* they are fleeing
is more important than *why*. One may say they are escaping
hybris, which here means simple lust. The word *hybris* is
used throughout *The Suppliant Maidens* to describe the
sons of Aegyptus. This does not, of course, mean that they
are overproud and aspire to more than human stature. On
the contrary, what they want is perfectly obvious and completely human. The sons of Aegyptus desire the daughters
of Danaus. Bold and unabashed, the sons make this known
to them. The daughters, perhaps only because of this bold-
ness, do not want them. The sons will use force if they do
not win consent. The girls fly; the men pursue. That is
what *hybris* means in this play, and that is all it means.

But in the legends of Greece, young girls are not usually
represented as detesting the very idea of marriage. Aeschylus
seems at times to feel the modern critic tugging at his

---

[4] Line 1002, marked regularly in texts as corrupt, reads

κάλωρα κωλύουσαν θωσμένην ἐρῶ.

κάλωρα and the first form for θωσμένην (for which θωσμένειν is a variant)
are not attested in Liddell and Scott, unless this be, θῶσθαι · δαίνυσθαι κτλ.
from Hesychius. Keeping one sound word, κωλύουσαν, I am led to suppose
that something has been obstructing entry to the orchard, whatever the
unknown words may mean. Hence my general, though flimsy, translation.

elbow and saying: "Drama has to have motivation." Sooner or later, the King must ask the girls (not Danaus, who stands by) *why* they are running from their cousins. They answer (335–42):

So I may not be bonded to the sons of Aegyptus.

You mean you hate them, or is there something unlawful in it?

Who would buy men to possess them who are close in blood?

Why, that is the way families build up their strength.

Yes, and divorce is easy when there's disappointment.

Well then: what must I do to satisfy your rights?

Not surrender us to the sons of Aegyptus when they claim us.

That is much to ask: it means taking on a new war.

The question is asked, but not answered, swallowed up instead in this problem of private right versus public interest which dominates the suppliant play. A couple of false issues are raised: that cousins are too easily divorced, must offer dowry, fill a subordinate position. Plainly, at least, nothing is unlawful: children of brothers can marry, in Greece or in Egypt.[5] When the King asked his question, they should have said: "There is nothing unlawful: but we hate them." For this hatred is necessary; without it there is no play, just as there is no play unless Danaus has exactly the same (rather large) number of daughters as Aegyptus has sons, that each son desires one and only one daughter, that no two sons desire the same daughter. This, if we may borrow Aristotle's way of speaking, could be called the

[5] See Thomson, *Aeschylus and Athens*, pp. 301–306; this is valuable, but Thomson fails perhaps to realize that the primary given fact, for Aeschylus, was *that* the Danaids fled. This he must record; if he could also show why, well and good.

"plausible unlikely"; [6] but critics have not boggled at it. It is given and necessary; so is the hatred of the daughters; the only mistake, perhaps, was to ask for logical motives.

But there is a dramatic motive of another kind, and its vehicle is the poetry. The suppliant maidens arrive on Argive soil in the name of Io, once mortal princess of Argos, their ancestor. Io haunts the play; she is in truth a part of it, though she lived generations ago and is long since dead or deified in Egypt, and though she is not seen on stage but apparent mostly in the lyric. Io was beloved by Zeus. Most heroines of Greek legend who caught the roving eye of a god were, in Jane Harrison's inimitable phrase, "abject and amorous." [7] She was one of those who fled, and the chapters of her flight unreeled the wonders of the known world. But Zeus pursuer is Zeus savior too: he caused Io's torment, and he set her free; her descendants run from the male lust, but to the male (Zeus, or Pelasgus, Zeus's representative on earth) for rescue (348-53):

Palaechthon's child, listen to me
with understanding heart, lord of Pelasgian men,
see me, the fugitive, the suppliant in her flight,
the young cow chased by the wolves, high on the edge of the sheer
precipice, where she lows her call of distress to her herdsman
and trusts in his strength for rescue.

The heifer image recalls Io. Elsewhere, with Hesiod's image of the hawk and the nightingale [8] perhaps in mind, the image is of the weaker bird pursued by the stronger (58-67):

[6] *Poetics* 24.1460A19: προαιρεῖσθαι τε δεῖ ἀδύνατα εἰκότα μᾶλλον ἢ δύνατα ἀπίθανα. The relationship I have observed here does not exactly fit; while unlikely (if you stop to think of it) it is not impossible.

[7] Harrison, *Prolegomena to the Study of the Greek Religion*, p. 273.

[8] *Works and Days* 202-12.

> If there stands near one who can read cries of the birds,
> some native who hears our outcry
> will think he hears the cry of Tereus' wife
> Metis the queen, the pitiful
> nightingale, the hawk-driven
>
> who from the green and the grown leaves ever debarred
> mourns for her lost country
> combined with grief for the murder of Itys, her son,
> the stroke of blood from her own hand,
> the mother's wrath and her anguish.

The clearest combination unites sanctuary, bird-flight, and the Egyptians (223–26):

> take your places
> in sanctuary like a flock of doves
> in flight before the hawks whose feathers
> mark them as cousins also. The enemy
> who would stain their own race with sex and blood.

Why, once more, do the Danaids run away from their cousins? *Why does the dove flee from the hawk?* Nature does not always ask why; it merely works. This is Aeschylus' real answer. And in the imagery of pursuit, devouring and embracing are much the same.

In *Prometheus Bound*, Io, who appears on stage, hates Zeus and would love to see him sent sprawling from his high throne.[9] In *The Suppliant Maidens*, the maidens recall Zeus pursuer, but he is Zeus rescuer too. The blame falls on Hera, though they will not quite let Zeus forget his own responsibility (162–63):

> Zeus ah Zeus, through Io's spite
> the gods' grudge hunts us down;

and if he fails them (168–69):

[9] *Prometheus Bound* 757–59.

Zeus himself will be caught
in argument that he is unjust.

The treatment of Zeus as a dramatic character must always exercise all students of *Prometheus Bound,* and to this problem we shall come in due course. In *The Suppliant Maidens,* he has not been commonly thought of as a dramatic character at all, but if he is less than that he is also a good deal more than a concept or an idea of divinity. Zeus has had his part in the action: to *some* extent, he hovers over it as does Io, here, or Atreus, Thyestes, Menelaus, Helen, and Paris in and through the lyrics of *Agamemnon.* Neither in *Prometheus Bound,* nor *The Suppliant Maidens,* nor anywhere else that I know of in Greek tragedy, does Zeus appear in person; other major divinities appear before the audience, but Zeus never.[10] Therefore, he must always, not only in *Prometheus Bound,* be seen through the visions of others. In *The Suppliant Maidens,* it is the Chorus of Danaids who present Zeus, as well as Io. *They* are interested in nothing but their own cause: this involves of course Zeus-ancestor, Zeus the guest-god, Zeus-savior, since it is Zeus in these aspects who is apposite to their situation. Then, the Zeus who is invoked to smite the armada of the Egyptian pursuers is no other than Zeus the sky-weather-god, whose thunders are the very stuff of Aeschylean lyric. The situation is unfinished; the end of action unseen. The very doubt of the Danaids, with their ignoble self-interest, ignites lines which celebrate a Zeus still more majestic than the thunder-god, Zeus the supreme mind (83–103):

[10] Aphrodite, Apollo, Artemis, Athene, Dionysus, Hermes, and Poseidon appear in extant tragedy. Demeter appeared in Sophocles' lost *Triptolemus* (frgs. 597–99, Pearson); see also Pearson's remarks on p. 240. Hera appeared, disguised, in the lost *Xantriae* of Aeschylus (frg. 168, Nauck-84, Smyth); see Plato *Republic* ii.381D; also, *The Oxyrhynchus Papyri,* XVIII, no. 2164, though this adds nothing positive. I do not find Hades nor Ares in tragedy.

Even for those beaten in battle and fled
the altar stands as a shield
to wrath. Spirits guard it.

May all come well from Zeus, come true.
What Zeus craves is not easily traced out.
It is a flame in the dark,
but the way of it is murky to the sight
of men, mere mortals.

What Zeus ordains to be an act completed
stands on unshakable feet and is not tripped and thrown.
Cross are the ways
and dark the forest openings of his thought.
None can see through it.

From the high beetling
ramparts of their hopes he hurls to death
mortal men, without
armor or show of strength.
Gods can do all things without strain.
Somewhere enthroned somehow he works
his mind's will from its own source
and its high station.

Fleetingly, the imagery of wrestling reminds us of the
concept of Zeus as the temporary champion among con-
tending champions: the Zeus of *Prometheus*. This is not
elaborated here, for the maidens do not want a temporary
chief, nor again a constitutional king, but an absolute
oriental monarch. The issue of monarchy versus democracy
(which is also female versus male, barbarian versus Greek)
is knitted into the suppliant situation which is the dramatic
action of the play. Zeus-absolute is the club with which the
Danaids try to beat aside the hesitations of the democrati-
cally minded Pelasgus. He tells them (365–69):

It is not before my own house that you sit and plead.
But if the common polity is stained with wrong,

it must be the people in common who work out the cure.
I will promise you nothing in advance. I shall
take up these matters with the whole community.

They answer (370–75):

You are the city, you are the public.
You preside. None shall judge you.
You control the altar, the land's hearth.
The nod of your head is the only vote.
Yours the one sceptre, the one throne. Yours all
action. Yours to repel suffering.

There never was a king in Greece like that.[11] The Danaids
get their way, but on Greek terms. The decisive turn of the
action, that is, the acceptance of the Danaids by Argos,
comes on the heels of their highest exaltation of Zeus
(595–99):

who sits beneath the authority of no one
nor sways a lesser power under those greater.
No force is set above him which he must obey.
The action with the word is his
to make true, where mind and will desire it.

But note the terms in which Danaus reports the Argive
answer (600–601):

Courage my children: all in this city has gone well.
The people have acted, and their ballot has full force.

We hear, now, not what the Argive king decreed, but how
the air bristled with the raised hands of the voters, after
the King's speech of persuasion.

[11] For Greek tragedy, the apparent exception is Sophocles' Theseus in
Oedipus at Colonus. He needs to be reminded by Oedipus that adoption of
the suppliant may mean trouble, line 589; he decides promptly and without
consultation to adopt him, lines 636–37. See also above, note 3. But the
character and part of Theseus seem to be shaped more as for an executive
who can act promptly without encumbrance than for a representative of
monarchy. It is safer to make Sophocles nonpolitical than to make him
anti-democratic, despite the irritable self-sufficiency of his tyrant figures.

The assertion of Zeus-absolute should not, then, be taken out of context, as if Aeschylus had seized occasion to deliver to the Athenians his own concept of Zeus compact in a hymn (though he may be doing that too: motives need not be exclusive). The assertion of Zeus-absolute ends, rather, a partisan invocation by the Chorus to their god which states *all* the issues of the play, from Io to now, from Zeus to here, which exemplifies all the uses of poetry in this play, best seen in full (524–601):

> O lord of lords, of blessed ones
> most blessed, of powers complete,
> most complete power, Zeus magnificent,
> hear us, and from your children drive
> back, in strong hate, the lust of lovers.
> Plunge deep under the blue of the sea
> their black bolted ships, wrecked fury.
>
> Look down upon the women's cause,
> our race, a legend of old
> sprung from the woman you loved long ago.
> Assent, make the story come well.
> Remember, oh remember, you who stroked
> Io with your hand. From you our pride
> of race, colonists from this country.
>
> I have come back to stand in the old footsteps
> where my mother stood, watched among the flowers,
> the cattle-grazed meadows, whence Io
> tortured by the gadfly
> fled crazed, bewildered,
> passed the numbers of the nations of men
> by destiny dividing
> the land in two, with the strait between,
> defined the sea crossing.
>
> She sweeps through the continent of Asia,
> straight on through Phrygia where the sheep pasture.

She crosses Teuthras' city of the Mysians,
Lydia with its hollows,
over the peaks that part
the Pamphylian and Cilician people,
the ever-resurgent rivers,
the ground of the deep bountiful yield,
the abundant wheat fields of Aphrodite.

Plagued and hurt by the point of the flying
oxherd, she makes at last
the fertile holy grove of Zeus,
the meadow that feeds snow, where descends
the spite of the whirlwind,
to the water of the Nile, unsoiled by sickness,
in agony of fatigue and the un-
deserved pain of the stabbing point,
and Hera's fury.

And the people who lived then within that country
shook at the heart with green fear
at the monster they saw,
a living thing, an enigma, partly human
combining shapes
of woman and cow, a portent to stare at.

Then who was it who quieted
the hard-driven, the hurt,
the sting-wounded Io?

He who has power through time unceasing
Zeus!
By act of Zeus' hurtless strength,
by breath of his divinity
she is stilled, her eyes weep
the tears of regret and shame.
She took into her Zeus' burden. This is true.

She bore a child, flawless
blissful and great through his long lifetime.
The whole earth cried aloud:

"Here in all truth behold
the seed of Zeus, the life giving."
Who calls this work the work of Zeus, our race the race
of Epaphus, will speak truly.

To what god could I with greater justice
and fair reason call, such are his actions,
himself our great forefather who with his own hand
and heart primeval planted us
and wrought, he whose favor is all potent, Zeus:

who sits beneath the authority of no one,
nor sways a lesser power under those greater.
No force is set above him which he must obey.
The action with the word is his,
to make true, where mind and will desire it.

The glorification of Zeus now falls into its proper place.
It is a joining piece, to connect the antique history of Io
with the present situation in Argos, where the suppliants
are trying to keep an eye on the earthly King but, simul-
taneously, on the King in heaven. From beginning to end,
the ode incorporates the themes of the play.

Women against men, barbarian against Greek, monarchy
against democracy, flight and pursuit, dove and hawk: these
are all issues. Then what of good against evil, or right
against wrong? The other oppositions warn us to beware.
The hate of the maidens for the Egyptians is given. We see
the Egyptians through their eyes, and the action of their
rapacious Herald. Does that mean a simple right versus
wrong? In the sequel this must change: the dead bridegrooms, the brides with daggers, will have reversed the
picture. The end of the play is provisional (1062–73):

Zeus lord deliver me
from marriage with a man I hate,
cruel union, kind Zeus

who freed Io from her pain,
who laid his healer's hand upon her
and made force work for good.

Let him now give success
to women. Better than worse
is all I ask, two thirds of good,
that right accord with right
with my prayers that from the gods come to me
the means to set me free.

The means (*mēchanai*) were once the bands of cloth by which the Danaids blackmailed Pelasgus with the threat of suicide; [12] they seem now to be daggers for murder. In the name of Zeus.

To sum up: the accepted modern opinion of *The Suppliant Maidens* is that it is a crude, rudimentary drama with beautiful choruses. This view is correct. In itself, it justifies an examination of the lyric qualities, as such. But when and if it is assumed that the choruses are something different from the drama, then I do not agree. To say that the action is padded out by lyric would be to put the cart before the horse. Lyric, rather, is elaborated tentatively with activity. The stuff of the story is simple and perhaps if given in summary not even very interesting—the same could be said of many powerful plays; the story only compels because of the dimensions, depths, intensities the dramatist confers on it. Another tragic poet might have complicated and developed the character of the principals, the tropes and suspenses of the action, the social and theological issues involved; Aeschylus brought the unseen, the not-present, remote persons and places, even the gods, into the dramatic activity, through the language, which is the poetry.

[12] Line 459.

II

AESCHYLUS

The Persians

The Seven against Thebes

Prometheus Bound

I SAW, in the dramatic technique of *The Suppliant Maidens,* in the simple action played out before the audience, a means of making the speakers enact on a larger scale the scenes and events of a far larger action. The variations of this technique are to be found in all the plays of Aeschylus. But the variations are infinite in principle, and extensive in the seven extant tragedies. The body of material from which the dramatic story is drawn, the shape of the story itself, and its place in its trilogy, all bear on this.

The regular fund of dramatic story is the Greek heroic period, the interconnected legends once dealt with in the Epic Cycle, the few generations (mostly) before, during, and after the Trojan War. In *Agamemnon*, the first play of the *Oresteia*, Aeschylus saw the whole background of the Trojan War in choral and reminiscent glances, building the substructure for the play's single act, the murder of Agamemnon. The second and third dramas of the trilogy can thus be more compact and concentrated in relation to the immediate action; and *The Libation Bearers* can even show in simple form the kind of intrigue and dramatic deception which will become the stuff of Sophoclean tragedy. *The Seven against Thebes*, also from the heroic saga cycle, involves a single, massive design, a genuine story shape or pattern. *Prometheus Bound* goes back to a time before the heroic age, to the beginning of the history of the world as we understand the world. Gods dominate the stage, and human beings, except for irrational Io, are only a theme for rage in heaven, with no history yet, but a future. In *The Persians*, Aeschylus, by special privilege or in bold experiment, makes a drama out of the history of the immediate past, though he keeps the tragic convention in naming no living Greek and in bringing no Greek on stage, only the Barbarians, contemporary, but beyond the horizon, as remote in space as Agamemnon or Hector were in time.[1] All these plays exploit, but differently, the lyric presentation of scenes to the imagination.

The problem of *The Persians* was to dramatize Xerxes' invasion of Greece and his defeat. The real campaign took

[1] Since the date of *The Suppliant Maidens* is probably to be pushed down (see above, Chapter I, note 1), *The Persians* is almost certainly the oldest extant Greek tragedy. The conventions may, then, not have been absolutely fixed. Note that, even among the Barbarians, the only *named historical characters* are Darius (who is dead) and Xerxes (who is indispensable). I do not share the confidence of Kranz (*Stasimon*, p. 89) that "*selbstverständlich*" the name of Atossa was known to Aeschylus. Nevertheless, the rather wild list of Persian captains which replaces the true roster may possibly be due to convention as well as to a tendentious or defective historical approach. See below, note 4.

more than two years of action and nearly a decade of preparation. Xerxes bridged the Hellespont and led his great
army into Greece from the north, accompanied by the
fleet. Despite some checks and struggles, he continued to
advance until he reached Athens and stormed it. Then the
King's fleet was routed at the Battle of Salamis, and Xerxes
himself returned to Asia, leaving, however, a powerful army
in Greece which was not defeated until the following
year, and not until it had once more occupied Athens and
completed the destruction of the city. That was in 479; in
472 Aeschylus produced *The Persians*.

This was a theme for epic. How could it be staged?
Obviously, not through staging at all, but, through poetry,
making the audience see the action in reported scenes and
feel it in the emotional lyrics of the actors and the chorus.

In the first place, Aeschylus did not here follow the
custom [2] of composing a trilogy out of three interdependent
tragedies. The lost plays which accompanied *The Persians*
may have anticipated it in themes and moods and morals,
but they certainly neither initiated nor continued the story. [3]
The Persians is an independent tragedy, like the surviving
plays of Sophocles. Aeschylus further intensified the unity
(in the teeth of history) [4] by making one single action in

[2] Always supposing the custom was already there.

[3] The set consisted of *Phineus, The Persians, Glaucus (Potnieus)*, and
Prometheus (Pyrkaeus); Argument to *The Persians*, see Smyth, p. 377.
Whatever the connections of theme and imagery (and there may have been
none) these could not constitute a chronological sequence.

[4] See my article, "Aeschylus on the Defeat of Xerxes," in *Classical Studies
in Honor of William Abbott Oldfather*, pp. 82–93. Since, however, this
volume is not universally available, I may be allowed to summarize the
main conclusions.

    a. The lists of Persian names and commands in Aeschylus are sharply
      different from those in Herodotus. Those in Herodotus are coherent,
      those in Aeschylus incoherent, though many of the names themselves
      may be valid. Those who, like Kranz (*Stasimon*, pp. 88–98), have
      studied the Persian account of Aeschylus without a constant check

the campaign—the navy's defeat at Salamis—represent the
one great defeat of Persia which destroyed all. The Chorus
of Persian elder counselors open the play. They describe,
in a mood that combines pride and foreboding, the great
host and the great captains who have gone forth. To them
enters the Dowager Queen, Xerxes' mother, who confides
a dream of disaster. A Messenger from the Persian expedition arrives; he announces the defeat of the Persians, describes the battle of Salamis and the Persian losses in the
battle itself and in the subsequent retreat. He goes, his
message told. Chorus and Queen invoke the spirit of
Darius, Xerxes' great father. He rises above his grave, is
told of the disaster, reads it as the fulfilment of divine warnings, prophesies the defeat of the remaining army at
Plataea, and warns his people against future wars with
Greece. Xerxes himself then arrives. He has, really, no news
to add to the Messenger's tale. He and the Chorus make
an antiphonal lament to end the play.

Plainly, this drama is mostly *about* not what the characters and chorus do, but what they are told, and how they
feel at the telling. Narrative-exposition and lament (sometimes combined) played against tableau compose the bulk
of the play. Thus, along with the Chorus, the chief person

> against Herodotus have given a too favorable impression of the former
> as an authority.
> b. The lists, the battle account, and the arrangement of actions in the
> play have the effect of making the Battle of Salamis destroy the
> *entire Persian Expeditionary Force*, not merely the fleet but the flower
> and bulk of the land army. To this end, the minor engagement of
> Psyttalia was magnified into a major land battle.

I still think these conclusions stand. I also argued that the purpose of
Aeschylus was "patriotic," that is, to exaggerate the great Athenian battle
of the war. Analysis of the play from the dramatic point of view has,
however, made me realize that I underestimated the dramatic necessity of
reducing the defeat of Xerxes to a single major action. Motives need not
be exclusive. In this case, as rarely happens, the artist and the propagandist
seem to be one.

is the Messenger. Messengers are not peculiar to Greek tragedy, and not all Greek tragic messengers are alike in makeup and function. All sorts of characters can act as messenger; but the messenger in his purest essence is a person who is *in himself* nothing important or interesting, nothing to distract from the story he has to tell, which is all important.[5] He is thus, like the chorus itself, a personal

[5] The purest type of messenger is the anonymous character (normally a servant or soldier) who announces the catastrophe or decisive turn of the action. Murray ("Excursus," p. 343; see also pp. 354–59) would link it to the *pathos* of the Spirit. The report in *The Persians* is the best example in Aeschylus. In Sophocles, the pure messenger may be illustrated in *Antigone* 1192–1243, as contrasted with the *phylax* (249–77, 407–40); on the other hand, the *exangelos* of 1278–1316 (second catastrophe) is the same man as our *angelos*-proper or pure messenger, renamed because he announces what has happened inside the house, a distinction which does not concern us here. The formal messenger-speech is best exemplified in Euripides; he also offers the oddest case, the Phrygian of *Orestes* (1369–1502), whom Murray (p. 355) has correctly labeled *exangelos*.

Occasionally, a regular character of the drama acts as messenger, as do Danaus, in Aeschylus' *The Suppliant Maidens* 605–24; and Hyllus, in Sophocles' *The Women of Trachis* 749–812, a full, formal account, but prefaced by a sort of author's apology in line 749. On the other hand, some characters called *angelos* do not properly function as dramatic messenger, e.g., the Corinthian Shepherd of *Oedipus Tyrannus* 924—although he does have a message!

What shall we make of such a person as the *angelos* of Sophocles' *Ajax* 719–814? To refuse to call him a "pure messenger" might seem to be fussing over terms; he reports, however, not the catastrophe but, like the *phylax* in *Antigone* or the first *angelos* in Euripides' *Orestes* 866–956, an event that complicates toward the catastrophe. The pure messenger, in *Ajax*, would be the reporter of the suicide, if there were one.

The messenger's report (in our strict sense at least) should be true. Our Messenger of *The Persians* guarantees his testimony, line 341; Kranz (*Stasimon*, pp. 89, 92) rather quaintly takes this as a guarantee of Aeschylus' own veracity. Cf. *The Seven against Thebes* 808, *Agamemnon* 680; Sophocles' *Ajax* 748 (not "pure"), *Oedipus Tyrannus* 1239–40, *Antigone* 1192–93, *Oedipus at Colonus* 1665–66; less frequently in Euripides, whose messenger, after preparing his hearers, usually sails into his narrative with a brisk ἐπεί; but see *The Bacchae* 668–69, *Iphigenia at Aulis* 1540–42. The frequent guarantee of truth makes the more striking that careful tissue of

function of drama rather than a kind of character; and his use is narrowly involved with that type or phase or portion which is descriptive or poetic.

The turn of the play, after which no further essential action develops, is announced on the Messenger's first appearance (249–55):

> O citadels of all the world of Asia, land
> of Persia, copious haven of prosperity,
> our much magnificence and pride is spoiled in one
> stroke, and the flower of all the Persians fallen and gone.
> Oh, evil to be first announcer of evil things.
> Yet, men of Persia, I must speak, unroll the full chart
> of suffering.
>   All the barbarian expedition is destroyed.

Here is the climax, and the drama has run scarcely a fourth of its lines. What follows immediately is elaboration, the scene of Salamis displayed from the hand of a poet who, no doubt, had fought the battle as a spearman on the deck of one of Themistocles' galleys [6] (412–28):

lies told by the Paidagōgos in Sophocles' Electra 680–763; no wonder all the characters in the play believed him.

I do not find messengers in any sense in Aeschylus' Prometheus Bound, The Libation Bearers, or The Eumenides. There is no "proper" one in Agamemnon; the Herald, Cassandra, and Clytemestra play around the function. Sophocles' Philoctetes has only another Sophoclean liar, the emporos. There is no messenger in Euripides' The Trojan Women.

[6] Aeschylus was in the battle, Vita 4, Smyth (we might have assumed this in any case). As a hoplite, his place would have been either aboard a galley (epibatēs) or posted ashore. Many of the shore force (but, from the language of Herodotus, not all) were ferried over to Psyttalia, and wiped out the Persians stationed there (Herodotus viii. 95). I, for one, cannot believe that Aeschylus was one of these; his account of the action on Psyttalia magnifies it into a major battle, with cavalry by thousands; there is some difference between a poet using his imagination and a rampant liar. Aeschylus might have watched the whole action from Salamis, for, in the circumstance, the Athenians could not have used all their infantry, but this can be documented only barely by the notice in the Vita.

In the beginning the impetus of the Persian fleet
held way, but as the mass of ships was crowded in
the narrows, none could help another any more,
rather, our own ships fouled on our own ships with brazen
beaks, and sheared the ranged oars all down the side,
while the Greek galleys, taking every advantage,
circled, enclosed, slammed, and the hulls of our ships
rolled over, you could no longer see the water
so crammed it was with ships' wreckage and the men killed.
The rocks of the shore and spines of reefs were clotted
    with dead
bodies, and every ship of our barbarian host
still afloat sought to row away in orderless flight.
But our men! They speared them, mauled them with the stumps
    of oars
and offbreak of the wreckage like a haul of fish
or school of tunny, and the mingled noise of groans
and high screams was everywhere on the open bay
until night darkened and the eye of day withdrew.

But the action has been completed before the telling,
and the play has practically no progress. It is rather spec-
tacle, seen and unseen, with its processionals and ceremonial cantata-groupings on stage, and with one catalogue
after another wheeling about the central announcement.
Thus the Chorus, in its first parade of marching anapaests
(12–24; 29–32):

> All the strength grown in Asia
> has gone forth, murmuring on their young leader,
> and not one runner, not one rider
> has come back to the city of the Persians,
> who went out, leaving Agbátana,
> Sousa, and the primeval
> Cissian hold, some on horseback,
> some in long ships, while the infantry marched
> in massive array of battle.

> Such were Amistres, Artáphrenes,
> Megabates and Astaspes,
> dukes of the Persians,
> kings themselves under the great King . . . .

> Artembáres, chariot fighter,
> with Masistres, the bowmaster
> great Imaeus, and Pharandaces,
> and Sosthanes, driver of horses.

This is only a part of only the first in a great series of catalogues; through report and through lament, we hear twice
more the roll call of Xerxes' champions;[7] also, the genealogy of the kings of Persia;[8] the stations of the flight of
Xerxes;[9] the constellation of Greek and Thracian places
subdued by Darius.[10] Hecataean stuff of genealogy, map-
making, and history is turned into poetry—poetry rather
than science; for the names of the Persians, if not fictitious,
are assembled without knowledge of or regard to fact, but
with regard to color and association and, as much as anything, sound, which makes resonant and realistic and saves
from abstraction the *idea* of the bulk, wealth, and popula-
tion of the Persian Empire.

The catalogues open splendors to ear and eye, while the
laments of Persia, not always a separate element but combining with name-lists, work on the mood (548–53):

> For now the whole land of Asia mourns
> for the men that are gone from it.
> Xerxes led them forth (*oh*)

[7] Lines 302–30, 955–1001.
[8] Lines 759–81.
[9] Lines 480–514.
[10] Lines 864–908. To these might be added the Queen's account of her
ominous dream, lines 181–99. One dreams sights, not ideas; Persia and
Hellas appear as palpably as figures on a vase or frieze. The import of
their struggle is warning, but its terms are shaped for the eye.

Xerxes cast them away (*oh*)
Xerxes made all the plan, and all was bad
for our seaborne galleys.

Xerxes enters as his own mourner rather than as his own
messenger (he has no iambic lines at all), and the play
ends with a long exchange between him and the Chorus.
Ten lines or so taken at random from more than one
hundred and fifty will illustrate (1030–38):

I tore my robes at the onfall of evil

Harrow, harrow

Harrow and more.

Twice over, yes three times over

our pain, delight of our enemies.

Our strength maimed,

naked of my companions

in the sea wreck of good friends

tears for our grief, oh tears. Go home and weep.

I have emphasized the parts of messenger and mourner,
piecemeal, thus losing sight of the construction. Indeed,
the big pieces of the play are arranged, not without art,
and I have so far not taken account of the Darius scene
which, in a sense, pins the whole play together after the
Messenger has come and—because he cannot stay and play
a part—gone. The Chorus and Queen invoke Darius from
his tomb. By question and answer he elicits the news from
his widow. He then predicts the annihilation of the rest
of the army at Plataea. There is a little awkwardness: if he
is prophetic, why does he not know what has already happened? He did know, it seems, that it must happen; he did
not know when. The awkwardness is expendable, for con-

sider the gain: first, an impressive ghost-invocation; second,
an episode to wedge between the exit of the Messenger and
the entrance of Xerxes, who cannot quite be stepping on
the heels of his own courier; third, a means of working the
Battle of Plataea into the account. The battle has not yet
taken place, and must be given by a prophetic or omniscient character, a ghost for instance. And, lastly, with this
prediction of Plataea, a way is opened to make Darius
thunder out the issues of the play—barbarian against
Greek, monarchy against democracy, and, for once, man
against god—in a speech where the moral imagery of Solon
and Pindar hovers over the soldier's language of brute
violence (807–22):

> And there the crowning height of sorrow waits for them,
> punishment for their sacrilege and their godless minds.
> They came to the land of Hellas, and they took no shame
> to spoil the statues of the gods, to burn their temples.
> And now the altars of divinities are gone, their houses
> torn up, pitched over from their bases, beaten to rubble.
> Behold, they have wrought evilly, and not less shall be
> the evil they suffer, now, and still to come, the springs
> of evil have not yet run dry, they still gush over.
> Their life blood shall be sacrificial, the clotted gift
> to earth at Plataea underneath the Dorian spear.
> Into the third generation the piled dunes of the dead
> voiceless shall indicate before the eyes of men
> that one who is born mortal should not think too high.
> For lawless violence comes to flower and bears a crop
> of ruin, and the reaping of it is full of tears.

In sum: the effectiveness of *The Persians* remains a personal matter, but the means to its effects can be demon-
strated in part. I find the Athenians wise in their custom
of taking the stories of tragedy from legend rather than
from contemporary reality. The Persian War binds too

much; the Trojan War sets the poet free. We can be grateful, indeed, for this exception which proves the rule. Aeschylus, indeed, works a strong magic, but it is magic; there is little real feeling (one can only be personal). Circumstances dictated an artful play of the Persian names against the nameless Greeks. But the incantation of the names is spell-binding and goes soft on analysis; and while we rejoice in the victory of Greece and freedom, these Greeks are far away and lost from the mind after the Salamis episode. Herodotus, idealizing them less, and enabled, as Aeschylus was not, to write from the Greek point of view, brought home their triumph with more force. As for Xerxes: who cares about Xerxes? Is there anything dramatic about a man getting so precisely what he deserves? (I merely ask.) He is in danger of becoming a moral proposition instead of a man; Aeschylus can rescue him only by turning him into sheer emotion. He weeps, and that is all.

The Persians works, thus, both against and for my contention that the poetry of Aeschylus makes his drama. It shows, perhaps, the need for a true character to sustain the burden, an Eteocles, a Prometheus, even a Chorus of Danaids, for these give a far better illusion of reality than Darius or his Queen, or Xerxes, or the Persian elders. But if *The Persians* is a tour de force, then what a tour de force it is.

And, lastly, what would it be without the poetry? Take the term in the ordinary sense: versification, language, rhetoric, sound. Turn the whole into forceful prose; only the eye witness report of battle and retreat would stand up, where Aeschylus, using the language of poetry, is still as tough and bitter as the best prose reporter could be. The name lists would be dull; the dirges—translator's despair—where even the Greek fails in cold print and needs sound and singing, would be intolerable. But take the poetry also as the means of opening the imagination to what, unseen by the eye and unheard by the ear, makes real and articulate the spoken action before an audience. Without this, there is no play left at all.

The Seven against Thebes (hereafter simply *The Seven*), like *The Persians*, revolves around an unseen battle. There the resemblance ends. Instead of having to compress a campaign, a whole war, Aeschylus here had an action whose story pattern simply generated the drama as he composed it. I find it thus possible to give some account of *The Seven*, inadequate though it must be, without extensive illustration.

The Seven was the concluding piece to a trilogy presented in 467 B.C.[11] Oedipus cursed his sons, who quarreled over the succession, saying that their dispute would be settled by a Chalybian stranger, a migrant from the Scythians— that is, the steel sword of the Northeast.[12] Eteocles drove out Polynices and reigned in Thebes. Polynices married the daughter of Adrastus, king of Argos, and led against Thebes an army commanded by himself and six other great champions. At each of the seven gates of Thebes a Theban hero fought an invader. At six gates the Thebans were successful; at the seventh, Eteocles and Polynices killed each other. Thebes was saved.

This is the simple core of the legend, followed by all who dealt with it. Beyond these fundamental facts, details, as usual, vary greatly. But there seems to be common consent on one point of interpretation: the Seven who attacked Thebes were greater, if not in prowess at least in reputation,

[11] The set consisted of *Laïus, Oedipus, The Seven against Thebes,* and *The Sphinx*. See Smyth, p. 377; frgs. 121, 122, 173, 235–37, Nauck. For details and variations of the saga, see Preller-Robert, *Griechische Mythologie,* II, 876–968.

[12] For the curse, *The Seven* 656, 711; the steel, 728, 816–19, 885, 908–12.

than their Theban opponents; the odds were against
Thebes; the Seven lost because the gods were against them
or because of some deficiency in their own characters.[13]
One variant belongs particularly to Attic tragedy. The
Thebans decreed that Polynices should not be buried; but
Antigone defied the decree and buried him.

Aeschylus' *The Seven against Thebes* spans the action
from the point of time when the final battle is certain to
the death-procession and antiphonal dirge when the bodies
of the brothers are carried in, mourned by Antigone and
Ismene each leading half the Chorus, and when Antigone
defies the Herald of Thebes and proclaims her intention
to bury Polynices.[14]

The battle of the gates is, of course, the central event of
this story, but Aeschylus did not, as in *The Persians*, make
the report of battle the center of his tragedy. The final
issue is reported by the Messenger in a speech of only
eleven lines [15] without details. The heart of *The Seven* consists of a long scene between Eteocles and one of his army
scouts, arranged as follows:

Scout ("messenger"): Description of Argive champion at Theban gate: his name, armor and shield-
blazon, mood and battle-vaunts.

[13] Opposition of the gods, *The Iliad* iv.381; Pindar *Nem.* 9.18–26; *Pyth.*
8.48–50. Disobedience to the gods and reckless character, *The Iliad* iv.405–
10. In general, see Preller-Robert, II, 933–36.

[14] It is frequently, perhaps even usually, held that the ending of *The
Seven against Thebes*, which involves Antigone's defiant resolve to bury
Polynices, is a late addition by an "Überarbeiter" who tried to adapt the
play to Sophocles' *Antigone*. See, e.g., Pohlenz, *Die griechische Tragödie*,
p. 91 with extensive note. There is no authority in the MSS. for rejecting
the lines, and those who see corruption have their usual difficulty in agreeing
where the corruption begins. Since nothing has been or can be said which
will *prove* that the ending is spurious, it is here treated as genuine.

[15] Lines 792–802.

| Eteocles: | Answer to the boasting and the blazon. Dispatch of a Theban champion (name, character) to hold the gate. |
| Chorus: | Blessings on the Theban, horror and fear of the Argives (exactly five lines for each). |

The first of these sequences will illustrate their manner (375–421):

I have examined well the disposition
of our enemies, how each is allotted to his gate,
and so can speak.
Tydeus is thundering now against the Proetid Gate,
although the soothsayer will not let him cross the ford [16]
of Ismenus, for their sacrifices are not good.
But Tydeus, lewd with fury and the lust for war,
rasps out in the dry discords of the snake at noon,
and batters the wise Amphiaraus with his abuse
as one who, faint in battle, cringes before death.
Such are his cries. He shakes three overshadowing manes
of hair upon his helm, and from inside his shield
bells beaten out of bronze clash terror.
And on his shield he bears a blazon of pride, that shows
the sky upon it, wrought, and all ablaze with stars.
There in the broad shield's middle is the bright full moon
conspicuous, night's glory, greatest of the stars.
In such a rage of arrogance on his battle-gear
he cries beside the river banks, lovesick for war,
a horse that gasps and rages on his curb
and waits the trumpet's signal to let go his charge.
Whom will you stand against him? When the bars go down,
what man will wear your trust before the Proetid Gate?

---

[16] The traditional adverse omens (Preller-Robert, II, 933–36) are thus made reminiscent of the historical situation at the Battle of Plataea, just twelve years ago. See Herodotus ix.36–37.1.

I will not tremble at the armor a man wears.
His heraldry will make no holes;
and bell and crest spearless shall have no bite. As for
that night of his you say is blazoned on his shield,
glaring with its skyful of stars, I think this foolishness
may be prophetic for someone.
If night could be the night that closes on his eyes
who wears on him such overmastering blazonry,
then night might answer truly to her own dark name,
and he prefigures his outrage upon himself.
I against Tydeus will send forth Astacus' son
to stand defender of these gates. He is well born.
He gives the throne of modesty its rightful due.
He loathes boastful talk. Slow to do shame,
he has no liking to be slow in war. His stock
goes back to heroes sown once of the dragon's seed
and saved by Ares. Oh, he is grown straight from this soil.
His name is Melanippus. Ares with his dice
shall settle the issue;
but Justice, his kinswoman, truly sends him now
to beat the hostile spear from her who gave him birth.

Luck to our champion now.
Gods give it. He goes to fight
nobly for our city. But I shake to think
of blood and death of those who die
for their friends. May I not see it.

For gate after gate, against Tydeus, Capaneus, Eteoclus,
Hippomedon, Parthenopaeus, the pattern is repeated. The
sixth invader, Amphiaraus, who wears no blazon on his
shield, is the one just and temperate man of the expedition,
in it against his will, a prophet who foresees defeat and his
own death, but who is carried forward on the momentum
of the drama; and so he, too, is given a Theban champion.
The seventh is Polynices, whose shield blazons his claim
in the painting of Justice (*Dikē*), a goddess, leading him

home to his city.[17] Against him Eteocles will go and fight. The decision is inevitable; so is the end. The Chorus plead vainly against the decision; the Messenger announces the end, the sisters mourn it, and the play is over.

Like *The Persians, The Seven* was played to an audience full of memories of the Persian War, its preludes and aftermaths. Then the blatant and showy invaders had been routed, against all hope and by the help of the gods. Then, too, the great *émigrés* of Greece had led the barbarian against their own homeland. In particular Demaratus, king of Sparta, driven out of his kingdom by his colleague king, rode back to Greece at the side of Xerxes, and at Thermopylae faced Leonidas, king of the other royal house which had driven him out.[18] Demaratus at first had been on the right side, and might have claimed like Polynices that Justice was leading him home. But in the end it was Demaratus who was the traitor, and Leonidas the king who died for his people.

Is *The Seven* a re-enactment of the moral situation in this and other crises of history? Not exactly. The analogies for many reasons can not be pressed home.[19] Further, the moral and patriotic issues with which the play abounds are

[17] *The Seven* 644–48. Compare Aeschylus' own adaptation of this, *Agamemnon* 910–11. Compare also Pindar *Pyth.* 6.16–19 (*Nikē* replaces *Dikē*); and "Athene" escorting Pisistratus home (the verb is of course κατάγω), Herodotus i.60.3–5.

[18] For the expulsion of Demaratus see, in particular, Herodotus vi.51, 61–70; Demaratus at Thermopylae, vii.209, 234–39 (his loyalty to Xerxes seems equivocal); Leonidas as successor to Cleomenes, vii.204–205; self-devotion of Leonidas, vii.220.

[19] For example:
a. If the Seven are the Barbarians, Thebes must be Greece. Actually, Thebes was forced by circumstances to join Xerxes. Thebans fought on the Persian side at Plataea, and after the victory, Thebes was besieged *by the other Greeks* (Herodotus ix.86).
b. The seer Amphiaraus, described as "one who wished to be best in fact, not reputation," according to tradition made the Athenian audience

subordinated to the mighty structure from which the action inevitably ensues. The base of it all is the brute fact that Thebes had seven gates. Drama and poetry combine because the action comes mechanically. If we ask, for instance, why the Seven fail, it might be possible to answer in terms of *hybris*-punishment; they fail because they are boastful and bloodthirsty. But, first, this will not motivate the death of Eteocles.[20] Again, their characters, valors, their identities, blazons, and dooms are all, with the *Dikē* of Polynices and the curse of Oedipus, subordinate elements to build the symmetry of the central scene: Eteocles stands with six armed, silent warriors beside him; the audience imagines each champion, outside, unseen, from the Messenger's description, and watches the Thebans go out, silently, man by man and gate by gate, until there is only one gate left, and one man to defend it against, and one man left on stage, Eteocles. Ask, again, why must Eteocles fight Polynices at the seventh gate? Because anything else is inconceivable. Because otherwise the pattern would be lopped with ends hanging and there would simply be no drama. Because Thebes had seven gates. Only a moralist or an Aristotelian need blush for these idiotic answers. It is

> think of Aristides the good, Plutarch *Aristides* 3. There is a better analogy between Amphiaraus and the seer Megistias, who saw destruction coming but stayed with his chief; see Herodotus vii.221, 228.3. But there is no proper counterpart to Amphiaraus to be found on the invading side.

[20] The *hybris*-punishment view can be maintained for the defeat of the Seven. These rampant assaulters were clearly the favorites before the event. Their own overconfidence, insolence, braggadocio, ferocity, impiety, gave them the defeat they deserved at the hands of less imposing, more respectable defenders. Amphiaraus, the one sound man among them, is swept on the current. The *hybris*-punishment view for Eteocles seems to me to be untenable. Certainly, he is overbearing, but no king who died in necessary defense of his country (even if his cause was originally wrong) could be committing *hybris, in any sense of the term,* and be punished for it. Would our Eteocles have preferred to survive and see his city beaten? If not, how is he being punished?

the senseless shape of things that drives Eteocles with a force more impressive than even the will of the gods or a father's curse could generate.

The massive welding of *The Seven* is sheer drama rather than poetry, if and so far as the two can be separated. But they can not be completely separated. For the scene of the six departing heroes could not be enacted without the Messenger's reports, the answers of Eteocles, the murmuring of the Chorus—without, that is, the imagination of the shields, the rhetoric of terror through imagery and painting with words; nor could it stand if not bracketed between the lyric terrors of the Chorus at the outset, and the lyric dirges at the end.

The date and context of *Prometheus Bound* (hereafter simply *Prometheus*) are unknown; the play would seem, however, to be the first in a trilogy which told of the quarrel between Zeus and Prometheus and their ultimate reconciliation.[21] In the war between the Titans and the Olympians, Prometheus, himself a Titan, went over to the side of Zeus and helped him win. Prometheus, however, then independently interfered with the status of human beings by giving them fire and thus the means to all the arts and the arts themselves. Zeus punished him by having him nailed to a fissure in the mountains at the end of the world. Prometheus still held a secret against Zeus; Zeus threatened, but he would not tell, and Zeus split the earth and plunged him beneath it for aeons, then raised him to be fed on by

---

[21] The best reconstruction of the trilogy is Thomson's in the Introduction to his edition, pp. 18–38. It has sometimes been doubted that Aeschylus wrote this play. For evidence, which is nil, and arguments, such as they are, in favor of this view, see Schmid, *Geschichte der griechischen Literatur*, III, 301–306, restating the theory developed in an earlier monograph (*Untersuchungen zum Gefesselten Prometheus*, Tübinger Beiträge zur Altertumswissenschaft, 9). The conclusions of Schmid, who is not the only one to dispute the authenticity of *Prometheus*, have been sufficiently demolished by Thomson in the above-mentioned Introduction, pp. 38–46.

the vulture. But Heracles at last set him free, and he was reconciled with Zeus.

Prometheus begins with the Titan nailed to the rock; it ends with the earth split to engulf Prometheus. Tableau and excursus compose the drama, which is, beyond others, "episodic" in the literal sense of the term, which means "having supplementary entrances" (*epeisodia*). Prometheus does nothing but consent or refuse to answer questions and divulge what he knows. To him come his visitors: the daughters of Ocean (Chorus), Ocean himself, Io, Hermes. Their conversations generate the long speeches which display before the imagination of reader and audience the scenes and stories that bear on the trilogy: the mutiny of Olympians and Titans, the punishment of Atlas and Typhon, the state of the proto-man and his redemption, the wanderings, past and future, of Io, projecting once again a piece of the map of the world. To this end, the friendly inquisitive Chorus of Ocean-nymphs, in the late style of "I heard you were in trouble and came to sympathize"—like the Trachinian women to Deïanira, the Corinthian women to Medea, the Troezenian women to Phaedra [22]—frankly prod the action along with cue after cue, though they turn heroic in the end and go down into the depths with Prometheus. And through all and over all, the speeches involve, in the poetry, the essential subject which is the play's one unity, the conflict between the displayed Titan and his unseen antagonist, Zeus.

Theme against theme in the manner of Aeschylus may be discerned here: intelligence against force, man against god, even, perhaps, Greek against barbarian, male against female. But opposition of ideas is presented, as always, through the opposition of persons. These persons are gods,

---

[22] *Prometheus* 126–35; Sophocles' *The Women of Trachis* (about 425 B.C., I believe) 103–11, cf. 141–42; Euripides' *Medea* 131–37, *Hippolytus* 121–40, and elsewhere.

not human beings (what Prometheus does always affects the fortunes of mankind, but he himself is a god).[23] But Prometheus and Zeus are individuals, not symbols or representative ideas. Therefore, though one of them is the most powerful creature in the world, his power is not absolute, nor necessarily eternal.

We are asked to imagine an age which—despite abundant anachronism and inward contradiction—is not only pre-heroic and pre-human, but pre-natural. The future of man, the world, the gods, the very laws of nature, are still pendant in process; they have not yet been determined. Only Pindar and Aeschylus, and perhaps Hesiod, could fully project such an age and world;[24] Aeschylus thrust such an age into the heroic period in *The Eumenides*, perhaps elsewhere, where to a certain extent we witness the making of gods. The concept of the world in suspense is difficult to

[23] For Greek accounts of the creation, see Preller-Robert, I, 78–87; for the special relationship of Prometheus to mankind, Preller-Robert, I, 92–94. There is no one full accepted account of the creation, and the origin of man is sometimes skipped in the origin myths. In Hesiod's *Theogony* (line 590), for example, Pandora, for whom Prometheus is responsible, is the proto-woman:

ἐκ τῆς γὰρ γένος ἐστὶ γυναικῶν θηλυτεράων.

She is Eve, with all her bequest of fascinations and difficulties. At this point, however, the *genos* of male men to go with the female women has not yet been accounted for, and in fact it never is in this poem. Elsewhere in Hesiod (*Hesiodus, Carmina*, ed. A. Rzach, Leipzig, 1913, frg. 2; see Preller-Robert, I, 84), Prometheus himself marries Pandora, and he fathers Deucalion who, with Pyrrha, throws the stones that become people (Hesiod, frg. 115, Rzach; Pindar *Ol*.9.41–46). Thus Prometheus ought to be the first man, but that is just what he never is.

[24] In Pindar *Pyth*. 3.45–58, Asclepius, the first mortal healer, is able to heal not only the sick but the dead; the unstated inference from his story seems to be that only since the blasting of Asclepius has the law held good that the dead must stay dead forever; see Aeschylus *Agamemnon* 1017–24; Euripides *Alcestis* 122–31. In Pindar's story of Tantalus and Pelops, the gods made Tantalus immortal, but returned his son Pelops to mortality, *Ol*.1.63–66. For the original close and cordial relationship between men and gods, implied also in the story of Ixion as told by Pindar in *Pyth*. 2, see Preller-Robert, I, 82–83.

express, if not impossible. Of men, Prometheus says that he stopped them from foreseeing their own destruction; or (222):

> I gave them blind hopes to live in them.

Elpis, hopeful expectation in the absence of knowledge, can concisely describe the human state, but for the state of the whole world where Prometheus and Zeus move as gods, explanation begets confusion, starting from these same terms (514–21):

> Science is weaker than nature [25] is, by far.

> Who does steer, then, with the rudder of natural force?

> The trinity of Fates and the Furies who never forget.

> And is even Zeus weaker than these?

> Yes. Or at all events he can not escape from what has been provided [26] for.

---

[25] I here venture to use the terms "nature" and "natural force" to translate ἀνάγκη, for which the chief definitions in Liddell and Scott are "force," "constraint," "necessity." Our word "nature" cannot be represented by any one Greek word. "Nature" as growth, for instance, is φύσις; "nature" in the sense we mean in such a phrase as "child of nature," or for that matter "natural child," could be τύχη, as in *Oedipus Tyrannus* 1080; but nature functioning as force seems better represented by ἀνάγκη. So in line 1052

ἀνάγκης στερραῖς δίναις

the meaning is that "nature" as the force of gravity compels the body which is flung from a height to fall, turning stiffly or horribly over and over as it goes (στερραῖς δίναις). In Euripides' *Alcestis* 962–94, Ἀνάγκη is Nature as the natural law that death cannot be cured. Of course, ἀνάγκη cannot always be translated "nature" any more than "nature" can always be translated ἀνάγκη. As often, there is no one-to-one relation.

[26] τὴν πεπρωμένην (μοῖραν or αἶσαν). Compare lines 103–105:

τὴν πεπρωμένην δὲ χρὴ
αἶσαν φέρειν ὡς ῥᾷστα, γιγνώσκονθ' ὅτι
τὸ τῆς ἀνάγκης ἔστ' ἀδήριτον σθένος.

See Boisacq *Dictionaire Étymologique*, s.v.v. πείρω, πορεῖν. What has to happen goes through "channels." The participial phrase depersonalizes

What is provided for Zeus except to rule
forevermore?

            Press me no further. Do not insist.

Here is some terrible secret which you hold against
yourself, and will not show.

The vital question is not fairly answered. The lines persist
in ambiguity, which is solved by putting "providence" off
on nonsensical, anonymous, unanswerable formulas. But
when Prometheus invites us to imagine the progress of
mortals from not-yet-man to man, we can follow him and
visualize (436–53):

Do not think through self-glory or mere perversity
I am so silent. No, but I bite on my own heart
for very spite, to see myself mishandled so.
And yet who was it but myself who found all ways
for these new gods of ours to have their privileges?
On that I will be silent, for you know it all.
Why should I tell you? Rather, listen to the pains
that men had, how I found them without minds
and made them conscious, and able to use their sense.
I will say this, not because I hold mankind to blame,
but to show the benevolence in what I gave.

First, then, though they had eyes to see, they could not see
clear; and they heard, but could not listen; all their time
of life was in the shape of dreams; dreamwise they saw
substance confused and blurred. They could not brick
their houses to oppose the sun, nor work in wood,
but like a boiling swarm of ants beneath the ground
they holed as deep in sunless caves as they could dig.

In other words, this is the imagination of "mortals" (*brotoi*)
who are not yet really men at all, for whom the laws of

the unexpressed noun, for if there were divine *persons* more powerful than
Zeus, why should one who is bewildered in this infinite regress stop to
bother with Zeus at all?

nature as we understand them do not yet function fully or have not yet been fixed, who, like Plato's troglodytes, must learn to perceive before they can march through the procession of the human arts and sciences which follows.[27]

Similarly, though one cannot understand either the limitation or nonlimitation of power, one can visualize Zeus when he is presented as partisan-tyrant, as wrestler, as armed master. Cronus overthrew his father Uranus, and Zeus overthrew his father Cronus, but the fifth-century Athenian can see the struggle between generations more vividly in terms of an insurrection in the community where a new aspirant rises against the enthroned master (201–205):

When there was wrath in heaven and their civil war
broke forth and they turned one upon another, some
striving to pitch Cronus from his throne, so Zeus
might rule, while others fought them so that Zeus might never
be foremost of the gods.

There Zeus, like many a tyrant since, became "first citizen" [28] or "duce" [29] with the help of a traitor from the other side, namely Prometheus, and there he sits as champion against his former helper and all comers. Thus his servant, Power, to Prometheus newly bound (82–87):

There now, go on with your rebellion, try to tear
the gods' rights from them, give them to mortals.
                              Tell me, though,
can your mortals bail you out of pains like these?
Heaven is wrong to call you Prometheus if that means
Practical Wisdom. Practical Wisdom's what you need
to roll free of the wrestler's hold that pins you now.

[27] Lines 455–506.
[28] *Prytanis*, line 170.
[29] *Tagos*, line 96.

In *Agamemnon,* the Zeus who has "guided men to think" and "laid it down that wisdom comes alone through suffering" is also the Zeus who sat by as two great wrestlers contended, and met the winner and threw him down, so that the name of Zeus was cried aloud, by herald or congregation, as if he had been the champion at the great games.[30] More often, he is the armed master, supreme because he possesses, and can wield, the heaviest weapons. With such, in his rages, he can not only overthrow, although he can not kill, any divine insurgent; he can also wreck the order of the natural world. Prometheus visualizes this when the daughters of Ocean advise him to give way to Zeus's threats, as conveyed by Hermes (1036–53):

To us it seems what Hermes says is well advised.
He urges you to put your obstinacy away
and look for prudence and good counsel. Oh, give in.
It is shame when one who is wise sticks fast in his mistake.

I knew already the whole announcement
this creature buzzes with. Nothing is amiss
when enemy hurts enemy.
Then let the curled bladed fork
of fire be thrown at me, let the air
convulse to thunderbreak and spasm
of brutal wind, let the storm blast
wrench earth from her socket with roots uptorn,
the surf of the sea main stiffening
welter the starry courses
through the sky; oh, let him pick me up
and pitch me over the edge of the black pit,
so my body spins in the force of fall.[31]
All he does will not kill me.

---

[30] *Agamemnon* 160–78.
[31] For the translation, see above, note 25. In Τάρταρον Aeschylus may see the cirque below the headwall of such a mountain as Olympus.

And this catastrophe of the world which can not be either explained or staged is enacted to the imagination in the closing lines of the tragedy (1080–93):

> No longer a threat now, it comes true,
> the ground rocks,
> the crash-echo of the thunder bull-
> bellows, zig-zags of lightning split
> and crackle, dust whirls in devilled
> force and the bucking winds
> from all sky quarters
> challenge and fight.
> The sky melts into the sea.
> Such storms, aimed at me from Zeus,
> advance, show clear, work terror.
> O glory adored of my mother, bright air
> who wheel the radiance all things see,
> you see me, and the outrage I suffer.

But if Zeus is supreme because he has the heaviest armor, then armor still heavier will make him no longer supreme (915–25):

> let him then
> sit high, hopeful and confident in his lofty noise,
> and shake the gasping bolt of fire in both his hands.
> Such armors will not save him when he must be hurled
> from his high place in downfall unendurable.
>
> Such an opposing wrestler he himself now trains
> to fight himself, a monster who may not be thrown,
> one who shall find a stronger flame than lightning
> and crash a stroke that overwhelms the thunderbolt,
> yea, burst to splinters the weapon that plagues the sea
> and shakes the earth, Poseidon's trident-spear.[32]

The terrible secret which Prometheus guarded was the possibility of superior power. The fate of Zeus, not only

[32] See Pindar *Isth.* 8.36–38 (probably 478 B.C.).

Prometheus, is still pendant through this play, to be resolved only through their reconciliation at the end of the
trilogy. Prometheus, true to his name, foresees it; but, like
the power of Zeus, the foresight of Prometheus is subject
to limitation (259–71):

Is there no end appointed for your suffering?

None, except when it shall seem best to him.

                                                 But how
will it ever seem best? What hope is there? Can you not see
your mistake? But to say how you were wrong is no
pleasure to me, and pain for you. Put this aside,
shall we, and look for some way to set you free.

It is easy enough for one who keeps his own foot free
of troubled places to encourage and advise
the sufferer.
                    I knew all this you are telling me.
I saw the error and still made it, I confess.
I was trying to help mortals and I hurt myself.
And yet I never thought I could be punished so,
so hung to dry upon the skyward rocks.

Prometheus claimed omniscience, but it lapsed, or he
acted mistakenly (*harmartia*) despite it. This is the agony
of the intelligent *man*, his self-fury when his intelligence
fails him. Zeus and Prometheus are both, after all, displayed in terms of the concrete imagination, that is, as
human: [33] and for all the fragments of deep theological and
even metaphysical pondering, *Prometheus* emerges as
neither a theology nor a metaphysic, but a drama of the

[33] On Aeschylus' treatment of Zeus in the Prometheus-trilogy, I find
myself in substantial agreement with H. Lloyd-Jones, "Zeus in Aeschylus,"
Journal of Hellenic Studies, LXXVI (1956), 55–67. Lloyd-Jones argues,
however, that there is no evidence for any change in the character of Zeus.
There certainly was a change in his attitude and actions (*Prometheus* 189–
95), and that is perhaps as far as we can go.

antagonism between individuals, one present, the other unseen, in the Aeschylean manner but also because Zeus
can never be represented in person but only imagined. Yet
again, the scale is cosmic; it is a drama of the world, and in
its incorporated poems the world is revealed before us. This
cosmic mood is maintained throughout, from the brief
scene at the opening when Prometheus, momentarily alone
for the only time in the play, protests to all nature (88–
92):

> O brightness of the open sky, and flying winds,
> wellsprings of running rivers, and o tossing sea's
> forever and innumerable laughter, earth
> mother, I call you, with the sun's wheel that sees all,
> see what is done me by the gods, myself a god.

This is nature—but nature only as it can be imagined—
since tragedy deals extensively only with what can be enacted, either before the eyes or in the mind.

There is neither time nor space to develop here the use
of poetry in the *Oresteia*. Elsewhere I have tried to show
how the trilogy is held together as lyric tragedy through
report, messenger, and stasimon, memory and forecast,
imagination of elsewhere, absent persons and remote scenes,
persistent imagery, and spell-binding. It is, I think, generally
realized that these elements of lyric do not merely embel-
lish the *Oresteia*, but are of the stuff of the action.

For the earlier plays, this unity is perhaps not always so
clear. At the risk of some confusion, I have tried to show
how the poetry is always the basis of the tragedy. This is
perhaps the only general rule for Aeschylus; otherwise, his
arrangements, like his stories, are not all of one kind: witness the contrasted shaping of *The Persians* and *The Seven*,
the differently conceived Choruses of *The Suppliant
Maidens* and *Prometheus*. For Aeschylus, however, we

must always think ourselves into the state of tragedy before Sophocles and Euripides and the conventions and shapes of modern drama which trace back to them; and then, perhaps, we can partly discern how lyric scene-painting, imagery, and lyric narrative were combining with the displayed character or group to make tragedy.

III

SOPHOCLES

Ajax

〔〔〔〔〔〔〔〔〔〔〔〔〔〔〔〔〔〔〔〔〔〔〔〔〔

IN 468 B.C. Sophocles, then in his twenties, defeated Aeschylus in tragic competition.[1] From then until the death of Aeschylus in 456, the two were active; from 456 until he died fifty years later, Sophocles was the acknowledged master of Attic tragedy, whose supremacy, from the aspect of formal award, was scarcely challenged by Euripides.

The first triumph of Sophocles was, it seems, scored against Aeschylus with a trilogy in the Aeschylean manner. How soon he began his own innovations is not known, but at some point earlier than the composition of any of the seven plays which have come down to us, he had begun to

---

[1] For the facts, see Webster, *An Introduction to Sophocles*, pp. 2–7; Pohlenz, *Die griechische Tragödie*, p. 170, with notes. The fragments of *Triptolemus* (which seems to have been one of Sophocles' tragedies for this occasion) are markedly in the style of Aeschylus; see frgs. 539–60, Nauck (597–617, Pearson). Whether *Triptolemus* was part of a connected trilogy is not known. It may well have been.

write, not Aeschylean tragedy in the manner of Sophocles, but Sophoclean tragedy. The principal change, with which all other changes connect and on which they may be said to depend, was to make regular a practice which had been used at least once by Aeschylus himself. Sophocles broke the trilogy. Under the continuing convention by which each dramatist presented three tragedies plus satyr-play, Sophocles now wrote three entirely independent tragedies, each complete in itself, instead of a connected sequence.

The immediate result is that the action of the play gains in speed, complexity, and coherence. It means, on the other hand, that what makes Aeschylus' tragedy what it is, must be sacrificed, that is, the dimension in space, time, and scene. Zeus and nature, ancestors long dead, heroes and heroines who never enter the stage, can no longer dominate the action as they did in *The Suppliant Maidens* or the *Oresteia*, nor can the map of the world and the peoples of its edges enrich the seen tableau. Material is jealously screened. In *The Women of Trachis* (or *Heracles' End*) attention is narrowed to the dominant theme: the destruction of the indestructible man by the gift of an enemy and the hand of a weak woman. The economy blocks out the alternate legends of Heracles in Thebes, the other children of Heracles, Amphitryon and Alcmene, the Dorian line and the future of Hyllus; it virtually dispenses with the labors of Heracles, naming a half-dozen in nine lines, then breaking off with "and other labors I assumed, innumerable";[2] that is, too many to distract the audience to a play which is not about Heracles' life but Heracles' end.

The action in Sophocles, again, mainly concerns one or two or a very few individuals, not a group. "Sophocles," we are told, "took account of the characteristics of his actors

[2] *The Women of Trachis* 1101.

when he wrote." [3] Among the players, the actors now definitely predominate over chorus. It is well known that the story of Attic tragedy is the story of this gain of actors over chorus, though of course the trend has its setbacks and the process is not peculiar to Sophocles. The number of choristers was reduced, perhaps before the time of Sophocles; the number of lines given them declines, and the scope of choral lyric is shortened. The chorus can no longer be the principal character or sing any part of the main action; its weight and effectiveness depend, however, on the whole concept of the drama in question rather than on date. Morally, the named actor is built larger than the nameless group members, and towers over them. More significantly perhaps, the discursive, which is of prose chiefly, gains on the descriptive, which is poetic; or, argument on imagination. The techniques of debate, organized and specialized rather than initiated by the sophists, which so strongly interested Athenians in the second half of the fifth century, appear in such discourses as Creon's self-defense through appeal to general probability, or in "trial scenes" where the opposition necessary to drama takes the form of two debaters squaring off, attacking and counter-attacking point by point, thus almost necessarily reducing the part of the chorus to that of a mild and ineffectual referee. [4]

The ultimate end of such tendencies will be to eliminate the chorus-players altogether or to reduce them to a solitary shadow, as in modern drama. Is Sophocles, then, dramatic (or sometimes forensic) at the expense of poetry? Is he really working toward prose drama? These statements are only partly true. If I grant that for sheer quality and magnificence Sophocles' choral lyrics match the best of Aeschy-

[3] *Vita* 6, Pearson.
[4] *Ajax* 1091–92, 1118–19, 1264–65; *Electra* 369–70, 610–11; *Oedipus Tyrannus* 404–407; *Antigone* 681–82, 724–25 (cf. Euripides *Alcestis* 673–74, 706–707).

lus only in *Antigone* and *Oedipus Tyrannus*, I must grant also that Sophocles is the greatest Greek master of iambic blank verse. Again: if it were conceivable to take the versification (or, in *every* sense, the poetry) out of Aeschylus and Sophocles, Sophocles would suffer less than Aeschylus. But he would still suffer. For instance, in his adaptation of *Antigone*, Anouilh has made a prosy, pedestrian Creon who is far more human and convincing than his Sophoclean counterpart; but then, of course, Sophocles did not perhaps want primarily such humanity and conviction as defined in modern terms.

I suggest that the poetry of Sophocles is essential to the full effect of his drama: if essential, then as essential as Aeschylus' poetry is to his—since essential is essential. But it is a different poetry and we look for it in different manifestations, in different places.

Many critics, ancient and modern, have seen Sophocles stand, statuesque, at the very center and perfection of Athenian tragedy, to whose art Aeschylus is an introduction, his rudeness relieved by glowing poetry and powerful religious thought; and Euripides, a decline, his less compact drama relieved sometimes by sweetness and invention and humanity. With such a view of Aeschylus we have dealt somewhat; with Euripides, we shall. With Sophocles, the half truth or even whole truth has this danger, that if we think too much of the golden mean, the perfectionist, the mellow glory of the Attic stage who saw life steadily and saw it whole, we are too likely to credit him with negative virtues of restraint, and thus actually diminish him. A close view of *Ajax* will presently, I hope, show another aspect of Sophocles. But first it should be said that the orthodox view, if such it is, has been challenged in modern times,[5] and that ancient testimony also produces interesting vari-

[5] See the excellent account of the "classic view" in Whitman, *Sophocles*, pp. 3–21.

ants. Sophocles said of himself that after exploiting (or parodying) the ponderous manner of Aeschylus, he then entered a phase in which his work, all his own, was bitter and contrived, before finding at last the style which was most characteristic (or most suitable to characterization) and best.[6] Some critics have assumed too confidently that all extant plays, except possibly *Ajax*, belong (because we admire them so?) to the final phase; it is quite possible that Sophocles himself thought *Antigone*, *Oedipus Tyrannus*, *Electra*, and *The Women of Trachis* were "bitter and contrived"—whatever, precisely, that may mean. Longinus is more severe: "Pindar and Sophocles sometimes take fire and sweep everything before them, and then again, often, they unaccountably go out, and collapse quite miserably." Compare Plutarch: "One might find fault with Archilochus for his subject-matter, Parmenides for his prosody, Phocylides for his thrift, Euripides for his garrulity, and Sophocles for his unevenness (*anōmalia*)."[7] What Longinus means, we may perhaps find, though not often, in the extant plays: sudden lapses of taste, metrical for instance, as when, after the colossal dignity of Ajax's suicide, the Chorus of his shipmates enter, singing their desperate con-

---

[6] Plutarch *De Profectibus in Virtute* 7: ὥσπερ γὰρ ὁ Σοφοκλῆς ἔλεγε τὸν Αἰσχύλου διαπεπαιχὼς ὄγκον, εἶτα τὸ πικρὸν καὶ κατάτεχνον τῆς αὑτοῦ κατασκευῆς, τρίτον ἤδη τὸ τῆς λέξεως μεταβάλλειν εἶδος, ὅπερ ἐστὶν ἠθικώτατον καὶ βέλτιστον. Full discussion, Bowra, *Problems in Greek Poetry*, pp. 108–25. διαπεπαιχώς may mean "after playing out" or "exploiting," or it may mean, not that Sophocles parodied Aeschylus, but that his own work looked to him, later, *as if* it were a parody of Aeschylus. Note that ἤδη . . . μεταβάλλειν (present) should mean he "was now (finally) changing to." So Bowra, *op. cit.*, p. 121, but the "finally" is mine; ἤδη, a Pennsylvania Dutch "already," is not translatable into ordinary English. I would take this to mean that the remark was made, not at the end of his career, but when he thought he had just found his final style (which may still not have remained the final one). It cannot, therefore, be dated.

[7] Longinus 33.5; Plutarch *De Recta Ratione Audiendi* 13 (*Moralia* 45B).

cern in lines so blithely versed, they must almost be forced to skip as they sing; [8] or material faults, as when, after the double catastrophe of *The Women of Trachis,* these Trachinian girls, in agitated measures, debate which of the two disasters is the worst, which of the two they should lament harder, implying that their agony of choice matches the recorded agony of the heroes.[9] Plainly, at least, Longinus means anticlimax. He may have so judged Antigone's famous rationalization of her own heroism.[10] I can not be sure whether Plutarch meant the same things, or the same plus others, or something quite different. *Anōmalia* (unevenness) might refer to such lapses; or to certain passages where, by our manuscripts, syntax and thought do not seem quite to construe a reasonable sequence; [11] or again Plutarch might have meant that there are whole actions which have a peculiarity, a surprise, or even an inconsequence or mystery, to show that Sophocles is not quite the perfectionist, nor yet the rationalist, we insist on his being. I doubt very much whether this last is what Plutarch meant, though certainly he noted unevenness; but I find in some sort of anomaly, which is not necessarily a fault, the clue to the essential poetry and drama of Sophocles.

[8] *Ajax* 866–68: πόνος πόνῳ πόνον φέρει.

πᾷ πᾷ

πᾷ γὰρ οὐκ ἔβαν ἐγώ;

Compare *Philoctetes* 1169–70.

The metre of Ajax's own lines at 351–53 may be rendered

⌣ – ⌣ – ⌣ – ⌣ –

⌣ – ⌣ – ⌣ – ⌣ –

– ⌣ ⌣ – ⌣ – –

almost identical with the hippity-hops of Aristophanes' *Acharnians* 1015–17.

[9] Lines 947–49. Compare Euripides *The Phoenician Women* 1310–11, which has, however, a little more justification.

[10] *Antigone* 900–28.

[11] See Webster, *An Introduction to Sophocles,* pp. 154–55, and to his instances add, at least, *Antigone* 4–5, 905–907, both of which have elicited agitation, suspicion of corruption, and emendation.

My incomplete demonstration will rest primarily on two very different plays, *Ajax* and *Oedipus Tyrannus*.

After Achilles fell in battle, his arms and armor were to be awarded to the next greatest Achaean chief. Ajax and Odysseus were considered; Odysseus was preferred. The infuriated Ajax set out to destroy Odysseus as well as Agamemnon and Menelaus and any other Achaean he might find; but Athene turned him against the flocks and herds and herdsmen and dogs, by making him mad and working him into the delusion that these were his enemies. When Ajax recovered his senses and realized what he had done, he killed himself with a sword once given him by Hector, his Trojan enemy. Agamemnon and Menelaus proposed to forbid his burial and throw his body to the birds and dogs; Teucer, brother of Ajax, stood over the body prepared to fight for it; Odysseus, Agamemnon's friend and Ajax' enemy, surprisingly interceded for his rival; and the burial was allowed.

This is the version Sophocles used. Whether he introduced any material variations of his own, we do not know. The legend of Ajax' death, with its labyrinthine ramification of variants, is a whole study in itself,[12] from which I will note here only the following points. First, Homer in *The Iliad* either did not know, or deliberately ignored, the whole story, and created an Ajax whose character will not fit it; Homer (the same Homer or the other Homer) in *The Odyssey*, briefly noted the quarrel and death. The story was elaborated upon in the Epic Cycle (post-Homeric); but it may well go back of *The Iliad* to draw on those masses of saga and folk tale which predate and underlie all epic. Certainly, the versions exploit the changes on certain primeval folk tale–heroic themes, such as the related ideas of the greatest man in the world, the destruction of the

[12] For the materials, see Preller-Robert, II, 1198–1207.

indestructible man, the dead hand, and the fatal gift—all of which may be variously stated. In one version Ajax, like Achilles in certain familiar but elusive concepts, was invulnerable except for a single spot on his body.[13] With this will accord both the story that Ajax, too, was killed by an arrow of Paris, and the alternate story that he could not even kill himself until a spirit showed him his one fatal spot. In another version, he was utterly impervious to steel, but the Trojans killed him by overwhelming him under a heap of mud. This story, too, has parallels.[14] Sophocles will not have any of this. Yet his Ajax, who can only kill him self, does re-enact the story of the destruction of the indestructible man; only his own hand can kill him—using the fatal gift from the dead hand of his enemy, Hector. My point is that, while rejecting the cruder variants, Sophoclean tragedy is here drawing on and, we shall see, achieving nobility out of, the naive brutalities of the dark pre-Greek age, as well as adapting the childish puzzle or riddle that lies at the bottom of every good folk tale. And further, this primitive fund has not vanished altogether, but remains to darken the drama.

At the opening of the play, all the main events—except for the suicide of Ajax and its consequences—are already in the past. The first part of the action progresses through the inter-revelation of these events by the members of the play who fit the broken pieces of their information together until all know everything that has happened: a technique which Sophocles used elsewhere, most extensively and strik-

---

[13] For Ajax, Pindar *Isth.* 6.47–48 with scholia; also scholia on *Ajax* 833. The latter gives Aeschylus' version. The near-invulnerability of Ajax is thus attested as going back at least to the early fifth century; the story of Achilles held by the foot and dipped in the Styx cannot be traced to any source earlier than the first century A.D. See Preller-Robert, II, 1187.

[14] See Argument to *Ajax* 19–21, in Pearson's text; J. T. Kakridis, "Caeneus," *Classical Review*, LXI (1947), 77–80.

ingly in *The Women of Trachis* and *Oedipus Tyrannus*.
In the first scene after the prologue, the Chorus—composed
of Salaminian fighting men who are personal followers of
Ajax—have heard with fear the scandalous rumor that Ajax
has gone berserk among the herds, but they do not yet know
whether it is true: Tecmessa, his captive wife, knows that
Ajax has been slaughtering and torturing animals, but does
not know what it means. The pieces fit; and this makes the
play's first climax of revelation (221–22):

> O report intolerable of this blazing
> man. You make all plain. There is no escape.

But along with this combining of incomplete pieces may
move the idea of omniscience, involved in oracles, portents,
and dreams, or in prophets or gods. In this case, Sophocles
has made a prologue which puts the spectator or reader
in a position of omniscience from which he can watch the
struggles of the participants. The play opens when Odysseus
enters, following the trail of carnage to the door of Ajax'
shelter. Athene then posts him as unseen spectator to an
exchange between herself and the madman, who appears to
her call from inside his shelter, armed with his whip and
resolved to flog a ram which he supposes to be Odysseus.
When he is gone, the goddess and the hero state, respectively, the moral each has drawn from the degradation of
Ajax (118–33):

> You see, Odysseus, the gods' strength, how great it is?
> What man was ever seen more provident than this
> man, or more able to do all things the time called forth?
>
> None that I know of. And I pity him
> in his misfortune, though he is my enemy,
> because he is entangled in this foul madness.
> I think of him no more than I think of myself,

for I see what we all are: nothing more
than dolls who breathe, or empty shadow.

Since you see that, beware
of breathing any braggart words against the gods,
nor take too much upon you if your hand has weight
more than another's, or if your wealth is founded deep.
A single day can knock down, and again restore
anything man can do. But those who know their place
the gods love. They detest the evil.

The stage is now empty for the entrance of the Chorus
and Tecmessa, who combine to confirm what we, the
spectators, already know. The scene which follows establishes the plight of Ajax, first with the hero heard within
his shelter, then with the full group before the audience.
Ajax has lost his delusions and knows where he stands. He
has made a fool of himself, his Achaean rivals can ridicule
him with reason, he has disgraced his father and his own
high reputation, he can look for no comfort in his gods
who have turned against him, he can never go home. He
must find (470–72):

> some trial and proof
> by which I shall make manifest to my aged sire
> that I, born his son, was no heartless coward.

The noble man must live with honor or die with honor.
The conclusion is clear to all, though the intention to suicide has not been stated, and it is as one about to die
that he shakes off the pleadings of Tecmessa and addresses
his son, before withdrawing indoors or closing his door.
But after a curtain-stasimon, he reappears to say that he
will make peace with the Atridae and bury his sword. He
leaves a Chorus wild with sudden joy and relief, to whom
now appears a Messenger with the word of Calchas the
prophet: Ajax must not be left alone this day, or the curse

of Athene may destroy him; but if he survives the day, it
will pass. The Chorus rush out to find Ajax. Some manipu-
lation of props indicates that the scene is now changed to
a remote spot on the beach; there Ajax enters, alone, and
kills himself; and there his body is found and the dispute
over burial is played to the end.

According to Aristotle, Sophocles said: "I make men as
they ought to be (or "as one ought to make them"); Euripides makes men as they are." [15] One can not hold Sophocles
to this. We do not know when he said it, nor whether he
had his *Ajax* or any other particular play in mind. I use the
statement because I think it is, in a sense, true. How can
we square it with the Ajax of this play? If we have here the
story of the fury and death of a madman whose good character the gods have destroyed, is this not monstrous rather
than tragic? But if Ajax, through the main action, is truly
Ajax—sane, not mad—how can he, then, arouse any sympathy or interest in what happens to him?

First, now, as to his madness, two views may be traced in
the play itself. To the Chorus, even after he has lost his
delusions, Ajax is still mad through the first scene with
them and his family.[16] The speech in which he announces
his purpose of reconciliation represents, to them, a recovery
of reason. But this speech is false, or at least misunderstood.
He is then still mad at his death, and never sane during the
play. To Tecmessa, on the other hand, he is sane as soon
as he has lost his delusion and seen where he is and what
he has been doing.[17] This I think is the true view, or, if it

---

[15] Aristotle *Poetics* 25.1460B35: αὐτὸς μὲν οἵους δεῖ ποιεῖν, Εὐριπίδην δὲ
οἷοι εἰσί.

[16] See in particular 609–16, 635–40; but the madness of Ajax is understood through the entire stasimon.

[17] See, in particular, 259; in general, 257–80. It is true that the Chorus
here agree with Tecmessa, but they have not yet seen Ajax and cannot
judge for themselves.

is nonsense to speak of a true view from inside a work of
fiction, then that is the way we are meant to look at it.
Everything the Chorus say stamps them as a group of well-
meaning persons who can not understand their chief because they are ordinary men and he is too big for them. I
would add, too, that the madness of Ajax in the opening
scene is not so much madness as bewitchment, affecting
not the heart and brain but the testimony of the senses.
Athene caused Ajax to mistake bulls and rams for his enemies; she did not cause his intention to slaughter his enemies; that was Ajax.

But that makes it worse. Suppose we coldly consider the
case of Ajax, and see where he stands. He claimed the armor
of Achilles, as the greatest surviving Achaean; his peers
thought otherwise, and awarded it to another hero who (in
this play of Sophocles at least) was admittedly a strong can-
didate. And that is the total substance of the initial "wrong"
done to Ajax. Any other indignities or threatened punish-
ments were in the way of retaliation. For Ajax turned not
merely against his rival and the rival's chief backers, but
against the whole army, slaughtering anything that came in
his path and flogging what his bewitched eyes thought was
a helpless Odysseus. One need think, for contrast, only of
a later Sophoclean hero, Philoctetes, whose wrongs were far
greater and whose reaction was strong but temperate. The
Achaeans put Philoctetes, incurably wounded and sick,
ashore on a desert island and left him to die. He hated
those who were responsible and the whole project of the
Trojan War, but he welcomed Greek sailors as friends and
brothers. To the violence of Ajax, however, add also the
man's colossal egoism. His shipmates, wife, and brother care
only for him; he cares only for himself. He leaves them with
inadequate provision for their safety, being absorbed only
with the re-establishment of his own honor, which is his ob-

session. He is the enemy of Hector; his play seems constantly to echo scenes in the story of the great Trojan, just off key and to the disadvantage of Ajax.[18]

This person will not fit any definition of a "man as he ought to be," if by that one means a model, a pattern constructed by Sophocles to show real Athenians how to act if they wished to be good men in real life. But of course Sophocles never meant anything of the sort. A drama or any other piece of fiction, realistic or not, is not a gobbet of reality, and the people in it are not real people and not historical characters, and cannot be seen or analyzed as such.[19] Sophocles' "men as they ought to be" or, better, "men as one ought to make them" clearly recognizes this. One has only to view Ajax for the purposes within the drama—purposes which end with it.

From the beginning, sheer stagecraft has projected an arresting figure before us. After the blood-colored prologue, one may hate the gloomy giant, but no one can ignore him. Tecmessa's messenger-account of his butchery of helpless animals deepens the mood and builds sheer size. On his own appearance, the self-pity to which Greek tragic heroes are all too prone [20]—but soliloquy demands a certain self-importance if not self-pity—at least makes him human. The true stroke by which Ajax may win an audience, however, is not here, but in the long speech where he announces his change of heart; and this speech is extracted by the needs of dramatic mechanism.

The purpose of Sophocles is to get Ajax alone with his

[18] Compare the following, from *Ajax* and *The Iliad* respectively: 292–93: vi.490–93; 468: xxii.304–305; 496–505: vi.454–63; 514–18: vi.429; 545–47: vi.466–70; 550–51: vi.476–81.

[19] Persistent treatment of fictitious characters as if they were real has raised false issues in plays which dramatize moral problems, such as *Prometheus Bound, Antigone,* and *Medea.*

[20] See Plato *Republic* x.605c-d.

sword, before our eyes, so that he can fall upon it. This, within the conventions of tragedy and the progress of the play, is not a simple problem. The usual solution, which would be no solution here, is the expedient used by Aeschylus: a messenger reports the scene. Once a chorus is on, it is difficult and unusual to get it off; [21] and in this case, the shipmates of Ajax, who believe they are attending a madman, cannot plausibly let him go away unattended. Yet Ajax must be got off, and the Chorus must be got off, so that Ajax may come back by himself. Nor does Sophocles want any undignified breakaway after a scuffle. The Salaminian warriors must be convinced; hence Ajax re-emerges from his shelter with the speech to convince them (646–92):

Immeasurable Time in his long course displays
all things from darkness and then buries them again
when they have shown. Nothing surprises. The dread oath
is overtaken, and hearts hardened brittle-hard.
I too, who even now held on so fierce and strong
like dipped steel, have been womanized in speech
under this woman's influence, for I pity her
at thought of leaving her with an orphaned child
among our enemies.
I go then to the bathing places and the fields
along the seashore, there to wash the stains from me
and rid me of the goddess' heavy grudge. I'll go
until I find a place where no one else has trod
and there bury this sword of mine, most hateful steel,
deep in the earth, where no one ever will see it more.
Let Hades keep it, and the night beneath the ground.
For never since the time I took it in my hand
as gift of Hector, who of all men hated me most,
have I had any good treatment at the Argives' hands.
Indeed, the proverb men repeat is true, which says

[21] There are, of course, exceptions, such as Aeschylus' *Eumenides,* Euripides' *Alcestis* and *Helen.*

enemies' gifts are no gifts, and they bring no good.
So, for the future we shall know how to give way
to gods, and learn to give the Atridae what is due.
They are our officers, we must yield. But what of that?
Even the strongest and most awful powers that be
give place in their succession. Snow-massed winter yields
to summer with her fruits.
The gloomy circle of the night stands back, gives place
to day with her white horses and her kindled light.
There is the blast of the dread winds that lets the sea
sleep after clamor; [22] and there is the strong wrestler, sleep,
who slips his chancery nor holds ever what he has gripped.
How then shall we not recognize what our place is?
I myself only now have come to understand
how I must hate my enemy only so much
as one who yet shall love him, and am now resolved
to work only so much advantage for my friend
as for one who will not be such for always. Man's
companionship is no trustworthy anchorage
for most.
         But all this shall be well. You then, my wife,
go in, pray to the gods
that all the end shall end the way my heart desires.
And you, companions, keep all my commands that she
keeps, and tell Teucer, when he comes, to take good care
of me, and to be good to you.
For I am going to that place where I must go.
Do as I tell you, and perhaps you yet will hear,
that I, who am so vexed, have found deliverance.

Whether or not this speech should be called *anōmalia*,
it has certainly presented a problem. One need only look

[22]   δεινῶν τ'ἄημα πνευμάτων ἐκοίμισε
                στένοντα πόντον.

As I see it, the blast of the winds can only quiet the sea by quieting
itself (ceasing to exist), not by blowing (doing what it does). It is just
possible that Sophocles lost his thread. See above, note 11.

at the critical literature on the subject.[23] First, one caution. We do not, perhaps, have the right to assume a priori that poetry-for-its-own-sake and damn the drama is *impossible* for Sophocles. He was a poet, and poetry makes a wilful subordinate; it will steal the initiative and generate its own sequences, whether or not they make complete sense in the narrative or dramatic progress. I think this has happened here to some extent, but I will not press the point, because the speech, taken as a whole, does perform a necessary function in the narrative progress.

As dramatic subterfuge, which it is, the speech may seem overloaded. Ajax, in effect, lies. To do so, he uses one of the noblest and most cosmic monologues in literature. Ajax must think big. He cannot use a deception without having it grow majestic in his mouth; he cannot think of his own fate without aligning it with the forces of the universe. That everything he says deceives through truth, that there is a double edge to everything, puts the language into the oracular manner, the puzzle of daemonic dreams and portents. Ajax, while no less terrible than before and pre-paring for the terror of his final appearance, has assumed, also, the added dimensions of serenity, wisdom, even kind-ness. All this, and dramatic subterfuge too; because Sopho-cles could think and write nobly, we do not have to assume that he was not also closely concerned with the problems of stagecraft. He had to get his Ajax off. This the Salamin-ians can now permit, for they had thought he was mad, but now must think he is sane, and the audience, though they know better, can understand them.

But now the Chorus, too, must be got off, or we shall have to use that messenger. And after such stunning con-

---

[23] See, e.g., Wilamowitz, *Die dramatische Technik*, pp. 63–65; Bowra, *Sophoclean Tragedy*, p. 40; Pohlenz, *Die griechische Tragödie*, pp. 174–75; Whitman, *Sophocles*, pp. 74–76.

viction, it will not do for someone merely to come in and tell them that they are mistaken and Ajax is still mad and dangerous to himself. We need another heavy subterfuge, and we get it. A Man comes from the army. (This "Man" is, with some qualification, the anonymous messenger of tragedy. Note how, within the known framework of legend, surprise can still be achieved. The audience undoubtedly expected him to report the death of Ajax; but Sophocles had a better thing to do.) Teucer is back, and will soon be with them. The Man has seen him and has heard Calchas tell him that Ajax is subject to the wrath of Athene for the present day, and for the day must be kept safe. If, in a drama from the Trojan legend, one desires a character to speak with the authority of omniscience, he can quote Calchas or Helenus. That is what they are for. But even omniscience will not quite serve in a bare, brief statement. What we are given here is a ponderous theological statement of the whole issue (756–80):

For this day, and for this day only, the divine
Athene's anger shall drive him. So said Calchas.
For those oversized and insensate bulks of men
go down heavily in disasters the gods contrive.
So spoke the prophet; such a one, grown great in man's
stature, then thinks of himself as something more than man.
This man, on the day when he first set sail from home
was found mindless to the good words his father spoke,
who said to him, 'my son, strive to be great with the spear,
but always to be great because the god helps you.'
Whereto he answered, haughtily and without thought,
'Father, with the gods helping him a man can be
nothing, and still win great success. I trust that I
can still seize glory for myself, without those gods.'
So he spoke vaunting, then. And on a second time
when the divine Athene was encouraging him
to turn his bloody hand against the enemy,

he gave this awful, this unspeakable reply,
'Goddess Athene, go stand by the other Greeks.
Where we are stationed, none will break our battle line.'
With words like these he lost the goddess' love and won
her anger, for his thoughts were more than man should think.
Yet if he still lives on this day, we still may be
able to save him, if god wills it. Thus
the prophet spoke.

Sophocles sometimes writes as if he had been reading the handbooks on Attic tragedy and suddenly realized that he had left something out, namely, the theory of *hamartia*, or of pride and punishment, or of *hybris*, or what you will. In *Philoctetes*, after thirteen hundred lines of drama in which men make their own fortunes and the supernatural is not involved, Sophocles suddenly produces a theological technicality to account for the suffering of Philoctetes.[24] We find, however, that, after all, there is a dramatic reason; there is one in *Ajax*, too, and here it has been anticipated in the prologue. I admit to prejudice against the school of interpretation which makes divine punishment of human pride the main theme of tragedy; but I must point out that here such doctrine will not work out in the play. Athene, in the prologue, did not inspire the fury of Ajax; she turned it against the sheep and cattle. Such wrath, if it effects the death of Ajax, must do so by bewitchment, as by making him mistake himself for his own worst enemy. That is nonsense; Ajax dies sane. Nor does he view his death as an

[24] See *Philoctetes* 1316–35, where a real *hamartia* is followed by a purely technical *hamartia*. The reasoning seems to be this: whatever the gods send, men must bear. But Philoctetes has grown bitter against men over his misfortune, though it was only a θεία τύχη (that is, it does not have to have a reason). The effect is to make plain that Neoptolemus is preparing to give up his whole career of glory for the sake of a cause he does not believe in and a man for whom he has lost most of his sympathy. The pathos of the trochaics at 1402–1408 would be gone if Neoptolemus had a cause to fight for. The very artificiality of the θεία τύχη has destroyed that cause.

atonement to Athene. He does not mention her.[25] But the
speech serves not only to make Ajax die lonely, without
divine comfort, but to make possible the enactment of his
death. For the Chorus can not dispute a report like this.
They summon Tecmessa and all rush off, leaving the stage
empty.

Now, onto this emptiness comes Ajax with a great sword,
plants it point upward, and speaks his farewell to the world
(815–60):

The butcher stands there where he can cut most deep; if one
may take the time to reckon his accountings up,
this is the gift of Hector, whom of all my friends
I hated most, who was my manifest enemy.
The sword is fixed in hostile Trojan ground. The stone
has bitten its iron to a bright new edge, and I
have stuck it strongly in and firmed the earth about.
All is prepared. For what is left, you first, O Zeus,
as is your right, you I invoke. Grant me my wish.
The favor that I ask you will not last for long.
Speed me some messenger to take the evil news
to Teucer, so he may be first to gather me up
when I have fallen here upon this bloody sword,
so that no enemy may see me first and throw
me out to dogs and birds to feed upon.
I ask you this, Zeus. That is all. But I invoke
Hermes who guides the dead to make me sleep, firmly
without struggle and in one sudden plunge, burst through
the side upon this sword.
And I invoke those maidens who stand always near
and witness always all the things men do to men,
the solemn striding Furies, that they witness me
how I am treated by the Atridae, how destroyed.
May they, as they behold me fallen in the blood

---

[25] He did allude to the pacification of the goddess (not named) in his
earlier speech, 655–56.

of my own stroke, swoop down upon these kings, make them
perish, self-stricken, by their dearest and their sons.
Go, then, you swift vindictive Furies.
Drink deep, spare nothing; feed on the populated host.

You next, who wheel your chariot up the steep air,
Helius, Sun God, when you see my father's land,
hold fast, draw in the reins along the golden backs,
and to my aged father and the unhappy one
who nursed my youth, announce my fury and how I died.
Poor woman, when she hears the news, she will raise a cry
of lamentation loud through all the city.
Why do I spend vain time, though, over all these tears?
The thing must be begun and with a certain haste.
O Death, Death, come to me now, and push me down.
Yet I shall be with you below, and greet you there.

You last, o shining of the daylight here and now
and last of all and never again, you I invoke,
Helius too, the charioteer,
sunlight, and hallowed ground of my own native land,
Salamis, you who undergird my father's hearth,
and famous Athens, and all who grew up with me,
you springs and rivers of this land, you plains of Troy,
I give you greeting and farewell, you who sustained
my life. This is the last word Ajax speaks to you.
Hereafter, I speak only to the dead below.

This is the scene for which the play was made. It speaks
for itself, and requires no interpretation. But we can elaborate, if we wish, some of the themes which give their
dark light to the lines.

The suicide of a hero, so rare an act in Greek legend, is
enacted like the ceremony of a barbaric human sacrifice.
The standing sword is a butcher (*sphageus*) for Ajax, whose
bloody excursion made the inside of his house like a butcher
shop. But the butcher is also a priest and the priest (a king)

is a butcher.[26] Homeric sacrifice, which is the preparation of meat, becomes so much a matter of routine that we may tend to forget how bloody a business it was.

The holy sacrifice is made to and by a sword. In tragedy, the sword is often something wild and outlandish. Greeks had and used the sword from time immemorial, but in legend and history alike it was a secondary weapon.[27] Their true weapon was the great spear, used for thrusting only in historical times, for throwing but also thrusting in Epic. The Greek hero is a spearman. The easterner is an archer. But the barbarian of the north is a swordsman. The Trojans of Homer are so Hellenized that they fight the Achaean spearmen with spears as readily as they speak Greek, but even in *The Iliad* it may mean something that Hector in the end meets the spear of Achilles with his sword, or that it is Helenus, the fighting prophet, who kills his man "with a great Thracian sword." The heroes of *The Seven against Thebes* fight with spears, but the ghostly arbiter of the dispute between Eteocles and Polynices is "the steel of the Chalybes," the Scythian sword.[28] (A good spear could be bronze-headed; a good sword ought to be made of steel.) Sometimes, indeed, the sword is an embodiment of Ares himself. For Sophocles' friend Herodotus reports that, among the Scythians, sacrifice to Ares is different from sacrifice to the other gods. They make and renew a huge

---

[26] In Homer *ta hiera*, when it goes beyond "sacrifices" in a general sense, means the actual dedicated beasts who are killed and eaten. The priest, *hiereus*, is the sacrificer. For the ideas of holiness and butchery associated in tragedy, see Aeschylus' *Agamemnon* 735–36; Euripides' *The Bacchae* 1114, *The Trojan Women* 1315–16.

[27] Often in tragedy the sword is an emergency weapon, used where the spear, which goes with the hoplite's panoply, is out of the question. So Aeschylus' *Agamemnon* 1651; Euripides' *Iphigenia in Tauris* 296, 322; *Orestes* 1369, 1457; *Helen* 1601.

[28] The sword, 727, 817, 884, 910, 940; the spear, 959, see also, 585, 624, 676.

pile of brushwood. "Every year on top of this mass is planted an antique sword of iron, and this is the statue of Ares. To this sword they bring yearly sacrifices of cattle and horses . . . and out of every hundred men they take prisoner from among their enemies, they sacrifice one." [29] It is on such a great barbaric sword, so long that the self-sacrificer cannot hold it in his hand and stab himself, but must plant it in the ground, that Ajax dies.

Ajax has seen that his death is necessary by sheer logic. But the death is enacted, like the blinding of Oedipus, in an atmosphere of unreason, barbarism, primitive passion, where logic cannot reach, whose force we feel but can never quite account for nor understand. This is the dark substrate of Sophoclean tragedy.

We could not quite end here: all instincts of tragic poetry require a quiet ending. But also, the Chorus and Tecmessa cannot be left at a loose end, off stage and imagined as still in futile search; the dead hero must not only be found, but since his enemies are furious against him, his burial and restoration to honor in death must be guaranteed. One might still imagine, and prefer, an ending along the general lines of the ending to Aeschylus' *The Seven*: discovery, dirge, decree of Achaean Herald defied, defiance supported by Odysseus. Instead, Sophocles has chosen to give us a long final act in which Teucer stands over the body against not only Agamemnon but Menelaus too, before Odysseus acts the part of unexpected rescuer. The last scene establishes, one might say, several dramatic points which Sophocles desires to make.

On the irrational side, he makes use of one of those

---

[29] Herodotus iv.62. Sophocles almost certainly saw or heard this passage at some time, for in his *Oenomaus* (frg. 432, Nauck) he spoke of a "handkerchief of skin, Scythian-fashion," which presumably derives from Herodotus iv.65.1, only a page away from our passage in a modern text.

primitive horrors which hover constantly about the imagination of tragedy but are seldom if ever realized in full: the idea of leaving a dead hero to the dogs and the carrion birds.[30] In rescuing his Ajax from this, the poet, in rational mode, may have bethought him that the offenses of Ajax were indeed great, and that he needed some rehabilitation. In the person of Teucer, who has no force to back him but gives no ground whatever, we have an obviously congenial figure; such to their enemies are Antigone, Oedipus, Electra, Philoctetes, even the last Creon.[31] The enlightened humanity of Odysseus at the end is an effect obviously desired, since it is planted with care in the prologue. Nevertheless, the end of this tragedy is anticlimax. The more the characters reason, the more dignity (except for Odysseus) they lose. Teucer, too, who descends to Menelaus' level of mud-throwing, loses dignity, and the Chorus tell him so. But fortunately, at the last, Odysseus and Teucer restore some dignity; and, at the very end, there is a solemnity, which could scarcely have failed, as the great body is carried out.

The final act seems to incorporate some fragments of a political analogy. It is emphasized that Menelaus is a Spartan. Against him and Agamemnon, Teucer—born to the father of Ajax by a captive concubine, and represented as an exponent of the humble bow against the aristocrat's panoply (*toxotēs* means policeman in fifth-century Athens) —could only in a political way stand for the honest yeoman and the principle that kind hearts are more than coronets and simple faith more than Norman blood. But this Euripidean thought would have to be conveyed in the brother of Ajax, and if Ajax is not an aristocrat, I do not know what an aristocrat in tragedy would be like. The man of the

[30] But Polynices was so fed upon, *Antigone* 1015–18.
[31] *Oedipus at Colonus* 956–59, 1036–37.

people defends the man of blood against the malignity of Sparta. This, in fifth-century Athens, is political nonsense.

That is, it is nonsense if we press it. I do not much doubt that the problem of hereditary aristocrats and military heroes in Athens helped to inspire the play, but we cannot draw lines fast. Ajax has his own story and character, and it is not the story and character of any one historical person. In *Philoctetes* (409 B.C.) the legendary situation, the recall of the necessary man from exile, strongly reflects the historical situation, the necessary recall of Alcibiades. But no two heroes could be less alike than Alcibiades and the Philoctetes Sophocles makes.

When Sophocles had to choose between coherent theory and coherent drama, the drama won. It is the drama of individuals, not types. Indeed, morally, the dignity of the individual is the only thing I feel sure Sophocles endorses. I do not know his politics; but the dramatic man who will sacrifice the individual to the community—Menelaus in *Ajax*, Odysseus in *Philoctetes* but not in *Ajax*, Creon in *Oedipus at Colonus*—comes as near to being a dramatic villain as Sophocles will provide. Ajax is a dramatic person, neither a historical person nor a type. He is not even the insensate man of battle, opposed to the unwarlike man of counsel. Athene asks (119–20):

> What man was ever seen more provident than this
> man, or more able to do all things the time called forth?

These terms are reminiscent of what Thucydides says about Themistocles and Pericles.[32] Ajax is Ajax.

Ajax is no drama of ideas. The carefully stated moral is used to generate a nonmoral action; in itself, it works only for such a character as Odysseus, who supports but does not sustain the material action and is a bystander to its

[32] Thucydides i.138.3 (Themistocles); i.139.4, ii.65.5 (Pericles).

mood. Such a one can learn from suffering—the suffering of others. Odysseus does. But this is not Odysseus' play. It belongs to Ajax, who learns nothing, who dies magnificently and not as a punished sinner, who dies unrepentant, cursing his human enemies and ignoring his divine enemy with cold silence.

He is a man who would not be tolerable in real life. Who said that dramatic characters must be? Unless Sophocles really meant that he made people in plays the sort of people real people in real life ought to be—in which case he was wrong. Shakespeare's Lear, if he were a real person in real life, would have to be set down as a stupid, bad tempered, selfish, opinionated, conceited, and utterly childish man turned prematurely old by his own silliness. The action's pattern demands his greatness. The wild fury of the dramatic imagination, and above all, the lines, make good that greatness—while he lasts, in his tragedy. This is the illusion of poetry, which works here to guarantee the greatness of Ajax. When the poet tries to re-establish his greatness by rational argument, the pace is gone and the illusion fails, though the writing is good writing.

Ajax is not the best play Sophocles wrote. It serves, to me, to dispel the negative idea of a spirit of Attic tragedy who could do no wrong, and to replace him with the powerful poet who could achieve magnificence despite, even sometimes because of, failures and flaws. If it could be said of any play of Sophocles that this is not a good play, but it is a great one, *Ajax* would be it. But the flawless Sophocles is no creature of imagination or misconception. He is real (some of the time), and his greatness is not damaged by his perfection or near perfection. We shall try to see how he combines wild poetry and articulate dramaturgy in *Oedipus Tyrannus.*

IV

SOPHOCLES

Oedipus Tyrannus

But let it never be thought right that I should stay
in the city of my father, and be part of it,
but let me go to the mountains and live there, where stands
Cithaeron, called *my* mountain, which, when they still lived,
my mother and my father gave me, for my final tomb.
So let them kill me at last, for they destroyed my life.

Such lines, spoken near the end [1] of *Oedipus Tyrannus*
(hereafter simply *Oedipus*) after the catastrophe has taken
place and all is out, are a kind of Sophoclean *anōmalia*.
They are scarcely led to by the action; they lead nowhere,
for the drama does not even tell us whether or not Oedipus
got his wish, and there is no story we know of Oedipus dying on the mountain wilderness. [2] Thus the lines do not tie

---

[1] Lines 1449–54.
[2] On the origin, grave, and cult of Oedipus, see Robert, *Oidipus*, pp.
1–47. Robert finds his original home at Eteonus below Mount Cithaeron.
See also Pickard-Cambridge, *Dithyramb, Tragedy, and Comedy*, p. 201.

the action to the establishment of a cult, or annual ceremony, in the manner of Euripides. They frame no moral
precept. They seem, so taken, to escape from the structure
of a play which is fastened together with a special coherence
that leaves few loose ends, and none that are important.
The most popular modern acting version practically wipes
the passage out.[3] But it will be seen to be, after all, a part
of the larger action of the tragedy.

The plot of *Oedipus*, beginning with the prologue and
continuing through the next to the last episode, or act, concerns itself with the investigation of events which have already happened. It consists essentially in the joining together of pieces of information (*symbola* or "clues") until
the last piece has been put in, the pattern completed, the
puzzle solved. There are two principal problems: the de-
tection of the murderer of Laius and the discovery of the
identity of Oedipus himself; a manhunt combined with
what might be called a rescue party. But both searches turn
out to be after the same game, and the solution—discovery
—is complete when the two are identified.

Thus, the drama belongs to the general story pattern of
the lost one found. The lost one may be a lost husband,
wife, brother, sister, or any close *philos*, thought dead far
away but discovered to be present, unknown. A particularly
popular variant has been the one that makes the lost one
the lost baby or the foundling: the type to which *Oedipus*
belongs. Whichever variant happens to be followed, the
pattern of itself seems to generate certain features that are
required, or almost required. For the foundling story, we
may note the following: the child is noble; the child is
unwanted and is put away (usually for destruction) and

---

[3] This is the version of W. B. Yeats, *Oedipus the King* (London, 1928).
I have seen it acted only in the form of the motion picture directed by
Tyrone Guthrie.

thought dead; but the method is always indirect (in Greek versions, a servant is usually delegated to do the dirty work) and the child is rescued, sometimes miraculously nursed by animals. The child grows up in the wilds, and is thought to be plebeian, but is at last recognized by infallible tests or unmistakable tokens and restored to its proper station. Thus the story is in part a story of the triumph of truth over rumor or opinion, and the triumph is pretty likely to come after the darkest moment, when error is on the point of prevailing.

A brief consideration of *Oedipus* will show that it follows the pattern almost perfectly. The tokens are not used by Sophocles toward the solution—he has another use for them—but they are there in the form of those otherwise so superfluously cruel pins stuck through the baby's ankles. It is also true that Oedipus is believed to be noble, though of the wrong noble stock: instead of being raised as the peasant's son, he is adopted by the great. In this, Oedipus resembles Ernest Moncrieff, alias Jack Worthing, in his black handbag deposited in the cloak room of Charing Cross Station. The resemblance is important. From the stories of Iamus, the young Cyrus, and Romulus, to the stories of Ernest and Ralph Rackstraw, the foundling story is a success story, a theme for what we call comedy or romantic comedy. But *Oedipus* is a true tragedy.

The tragically fulfilled story, mounted on so articulate a scheme for comedy, accounts for much of the essential nature of *Oedipus*. No extant tragedy so bristles with tragic irony. It opposes Oedipus—possessed of rumor, opinion, or, that is, error—against those who know—Tiresias, the Theban Shepherd—the latter two pulling back against revelation, because they know it is bad, as insistently as Oedipus, armed with his native wit (*gnōmē*) goes plunging forward. Where characters themselves are not omniscient, the audience is. They know the gist of the story and can be surprised only in the means by which the necessary ends are achieved. They know, for instance, that when Oedipus says (219-20):

> I shall speak, as a stranger to the whole question
> and stranger to the action

he is, in all sincerity, speaking falsehood, though the falsehood is qualified in the term stranger (*xenos*, outlander): the stranger who met and killed the king, the stranger who met and married the queen, who was no true stranger at all. Or when, at the outset, he says (59-61):

> For I know well
> that all of you are sick, but though you are sick, there's none
> of you who is so sick as I

he is, indeed, speaking the truth, but more truth than he knows, since he is using sickness metaphorically to describe the mental distress of a leader, himself sound, in a stricken kingdom. Oedipus keeps circling back on the truth and brushing against it, as if he subconsciously knew where it was; the omniscient audience can only wonder when the shock of contact will come.

In addition to this irony of detail, there is a larger irony in the inversion of the whole action. Tragic themes may mock the comic by matching them in reverse. Bassanio's three caskets are Lear's three daughters. Bassanio, marked for fortune, chooses the precious lead; Lear rejects it because he must suffer. The triumph of truth and virtue in the foundling play is the joyful recognition: "Our Perdita is found!" But to Oedipus, Tiresias says (449-54):

> I tell you: that man whom you have long been searching for
> with threats and proclamations for the murderer
> of Laius: that man is here.
> Supposed a stranger come to live with us, he shall

be shown to be a genuine Theban, and will not
be pleased with this solution.

> Blind, who once saw clear,
> beggared, who once was rich, he shall feel out his way
> into a foreign country, with a stick.

The homeless wanderer by delivering the land from the
monster and marrying the princess became prince in fact
and then was shown to be prince by right, but this revelation turned him once more into a homeless wanderer. But
the wanderer, who had once gone bright-eyed with his
strong traveler's staff, now uses the staff to tap out the way
before him, because he is now old, and eyeless.

The reversed pattern shows again in the fact that the
malignant oracles have their darkest moment just before
they come clear, with Jocasta's (946–47)

> O prophesyings of the gods,
> where are you now?

echoed and amplified in Oedipus' typical tyrant-speech of
scepticism. Or consider the design of the helpers. The pattern story of the foundling requires a helper or rescuer: the
merciful forester or herdsman who refuses to kill the baby
outright, or who finds it and saves it from exposure (sometimes this is a wild animal). Sophocles provides at least
one helper, or rescuer, for every act. The appeal in the
prologue is to Oedipus, himself a rescuer (*sōtēr*) in the
past; and Oedipus appeals to Creon, who comes from and
represents Apollo and Delphi. It is as rescuer that Tiresias
is called, Jocasta intervenes to help, so does the Corinthian
Herdsman, and the last helper, the Theban Herdsman, is
the true and original rescuer. Those who do not know are
eager to help, those who know are reluctant, but all helpers
alike push Oedipus over the edge into disaster. Again, it is
the story as design which seems to dictate the actual cere-

mony of the blinding. The Greek word *arthron*, which means a socket, means also a piece which moves within a socket. The infant Oedipus was pinned through the ankles, the joints (*arthra*) of his feet, and while we would not speak of the joints of the eyes, *arthra* serves again for the eyeballs through which Oedipus sticks his wife's pins.[4] Thus the foundling-property of the pinned feet is ignored for its original purpose as means of recognition and transposed into a means of dramatic justice in Oedipus' self-vengeance, by which the strong man renders himself helpless as the baby was rendered helpless.

The fundamental story pattern demands precision in all detail where repeated words are positive, not suggestive, and nowhere else in tragedy is language so precise as here. Consider this piece in Jocasta's résumé (715–19):

> But Laius, so the report goes, was murdered
> by foreign brigands at a place where three roads meet.
> And for his son, only three days had passed since birth
> when Laius, pinning his feet together at the joints,
> gave him to other hands, and these abandoned him
> upon the mountain wilderness.

The lines are stiff with clues, which though they involve material facts (the three roads, the pinned feet, the mountain side), yet have holes in them (the reported brigands, the second-hand casting away), and they are arranged so that the clue of the three roads forces Oedipus to fix on the fight with the king, and ignore the still more glaring clue that should lead to his own identification with the castaway baby.

---

[4] See Liddell and Scott, s.v. ἄρθρον. For the pinned feet, see lines 718, 1032, 1349; see also Euripides' *The Phoenician Women* 804–805: Οἰδιπόδαν . . . . χρυσοδέτοις περόναις ἐπίσαμον; also frg. 557, Nauck (from the *Oedipus* of Euripides). For golden pins to fasten the (foundling) child Dionysus, see Euripides *The Bacchae* 97–98. For the pins through the eyes, see our text, 1268–79.

The plausibility of this, if it stands, is a case of the probable-impossible, or drama more perfect than actual life. The pattern story demands tailoring; and if this were a true report of real action, we could ask some awkward questions. For example: Why did the servant of Laius (Theban Shepherd) give the false report of *a body of brigands?* Why did he say nothing when he saw Oedipus in Thebes, but ask to go to the country? Why was he treated so well, when he had run away and left his master and fellow-servants dead on the road? One may answer these: he suspected the truth all the time, beginning with the encounter on the road, for he knew that the son of Laius had not died, and recognized him in this young man who looked like Laius;[5] he was loyal to his protégé, and perhaps disliked Laius, of whom no good has ever been told, here or elsewhere; the story of a body of brigands protected both him and Oedipus. These answers are plausible, but are we intended to work them out, or is there even time to consider them in the rapid progress of the action? This is not the tragedy of the Theban Shepherd. He is an agent, not a principal. There are other points of verisimilitude it would be possible but tedious to raise.[6]

But Sophocles himself raised a couple of questions which he did not answer. Why, if Tiresias was wise and inspired, positively omniscient, did *he* not answer the Sphinx?[7] Why, after the death of Laius and arrival of Oedipus, did he say nothing about the connection?[8] Creon's answer to this last is sage and temperate (569):

[5] Line 743.
[6] For instance, why had Oedipus never gone even superficially into the question of the murder? Some awkwardness is felt and shown in lines 105–31. Or again, how could Jocasta know *nothing* (lines 774–75, often and justly admired) about the stranger she married?
[7] Lines 390–400.
[8] Lines 558–68.

I do not know. And where I have no idea I prefer
to keep quiet.

But it does not take us far. Is it not, rather, that Oedipus
is the man who must find, and condemn, and punish himself? As for the question, why did Tiresias not answer the
Sphinx? Grant that it was awkward of Sophocles to raise
this, or the other question, when he would not, or could
not, answer. In this second case, the Sphinx is one of those
barbarous primeval figures who haunt the edges of tragedy.
An amorous [9] she-fiend who asks childish riddles and destroys those who cannot answer serves with effect as a
vaguely indicated background bogey, or as a blazon on
a shield by Aeschylus,[10] but scrutinized close-up she must
turn ludicrous; so, in the tetralogy of Aeschylus, she draws
the satyr-play.[11] But if the question *were* answered: again,
it was not for Tiresias to solve this. As Perdita is lost, so
she can be found; so the Sphinx is there for Oedipus to
answer. To say he was "fated" to is to overstate it with
prejudice toward the grand designs of heaven; but it is a
part of his pattern or story- *tychē*, which in Greek does not
mean "fate," "chance," or "fortune" so strictly as it means
"contact," [12] or, say, "coincidence," the way things are put
together.

The pieces fit. The missing one who has been hunted is
found. This is the special sense sometimes implicated in
the cry *iou iou*, the cry which Oedipus and Jocasta, and
Heracles in *The Women of Trachis*, give when the truth

[9] On sphinxes and sirens, both subsumed as types of *kēr*, see Harrison,
Prolegomena, pp. 197–212; on the amorous sphinx, see J. Ilberg, in
Roscher's *Lexikon*, IV, s.v. "Sphinx," esp. cols. 1381–85; in general, see
Robert, *Oidipus*, pp. 48–50.

[10] *The Seven* 539–43.

[11] Argument to Aeschylus *The Seven*.

[12] So at least I should judge, with perhaps insufficient authority, by
simply combining the senses of τυγχάνω-"hit" with τεύχω-"make."

is out,[13] the hunter's cry of Socrates in the *Republic* when the quarry for which he and his friends have beaten far bushes is seen to be grovelling right at their feet.[14]

But after discovery, Oedipus does one more thing to complete the pattern. He blinds himself, as reported in the one true messenger-scene of the drama, from the anonymous Messenger who gives us, not the fact of the ruin of Oedipus, for we knew that already, but only the cruel ceremonies through which that ruin is displayed (1251–79):

And how she perished after that I do not know,
for Oedipus burst in, shouting aloud, and made
it impossible to watch the rest of her agony
because our eyes were on him as he stalked the court
and ranged among us, crying to be given a sword,
crying to find that wife who was no wife, that field
that bore a double crop, himself and his children.
As the man raved, it was some spirit showed him.
It was not any man of us who stood close by.
With a fierce cry, as if something were guiding him,
he drove against the double doors, and from their bases
buckled the panels inward and burst into the room.
There we looked in, and saw the woman hanging, caught
in a noose of rope. But he
when he looked at her, moaning horribly, he loosed
the knot from her throat. Then, when the poor woman was laid
upon the ground, the rest was terrible to see.
Tearing the golden pins by which her dress was clasped
out of the robes she wore
he raised them, stabbed them into the balls of both his eyes,
crying that they should never more look on himself,
nor on the evils done to him, or what he had done,
but that their sight of those they should not look upon

---

[13] Jocasta, line 1071; Oedipus, line 1182; Heracles, in *The Women of Trachis* 1143.

[14] Plato's *Republic* iv.432D.

must darken, lest they recognize whom they should not.
To such an incantation, many times, not once,
he dashed the pins into his eyes, and from the eyeballs
the blood ran down his chin, nor was the storm an ooze
and drip, but there came both
a dark clear rain and clotted hail, and all was blood.[15]

What was the sword for? The question is left flying in
the air as Oedipus sees Jocasta, already dead. But why does
Oedipus blind himself? Students of motivation will find
their answer. So that the eyes should no longer look upon
the people, the things, that they should not. Sophocles says
so. He repeats it: how could Oedipus share sensibilities
with his fellow citizens, with whom he can now share
nothing? If he could have shut off the sources of hearing,
he would have: [16] thus making himself, we might add, the
outcast who was to be banned from the community,[17] because the murderer was to be that outcast, and Oedipus is
the murderer. We add this; but Sophocles adds that it
would be sweet for Oedipus to cut himself loose from all
evils, from all his life he knows now as evil; and then seems
to contradict himself when Oedipus cries for his daughters
and calls them into his arms.[18] But by then, the mood of
frenzy has ebbed along with the strength of fury, and
Oedipus is himself again, reasoning, and justifying.

Then, for the wildness of Oedipus when he stabbed his
eyes, could we say that reasoning of any kind is too reasonable? At least we can say that Oedipus' self-blinding can
be seen from various angles. It seems to be a punishment
of what is evil (*kakon*), for Oedipus does not deign to call

---

[15] The text is uncertain here, and I do not try to give more than the
general sense, which seems to combine blood (dark but clear) and fragments of matter (not clear, also bloody), the rain and hail respectively.

[16] Lines 1384–90.

[17] Lines 233–51.

[18] Lines 1480–81.

himself *kakodaimōn*, unlucky, ill-starred, but just evil (or
vile), *kakos*.[19] The evil Jocasta has escaped; the fury turns
on himself with, as we have seen, the formal mode of
transfixing those socketed balls of his eyes.

But blinding still serves one more purpose. The riddle of
the Sphinx spoke of man feeble as a baby, man strong as
grown man (walking on two feet), man feeble in old age.
And we have had Oedipus as baby, and Oedipus as grown
man, a strong traveler walking on his two feet.[20] We need
Oedipus old and enfeebled, and he is still a man in his
prime, and appallingly strong. Only such a catastrophic
self-punishment can break him so that, within moments,
he has turned into an old man, who (1292)

  needs strength now, and needs someone to lead him.

So he has lived the three stages. The riddle of the Sphinx was
the mystery of man. But it was the specially private mystery
of Oedipus. This—the Sphinx might have meant to him—
is the mystery of you. Solve it. *Gnōthi sauton.*

In this sense, but I think in this sense only, Oedipus is
Everyman. Stories such as these have shapes of their own
which force action rather than shapes which are forced by
reason or character; and hence, romantic comedy tends to
refine plot at the expense of personality, with stock or pattern situations generating stock characters.[21] But this does
not have to happen. Eteocles in *The Seven* is also bent by
the shape of the story but generates a momentum which
makes his necessary act his own. So is Oedipus. He is the
tragedy tyrant driven by his plot, but he is more, a unique
individual and, somehow, a great man, who drives himself.

Oedipus Tyrannus is a tragical tragedy despite its frame

[19] The word *kakos* is used many times in this play, but the most interesting applications of it may be found at lines 76, 822, 1063, 1397, 1421.
[20] Line 798.
[21] On these matters in general, see Kitto, *Greek Tragedy*, pp. 270–71.

of romantic comedy, and we should be slow to type Oedipus himself. He is an intellectual man, but not *the* intellectual of the time (Pericles or another). He prides himself on his insight and wit,[22] but for a man of great intelligence he makes disastrous mistakes. Partly, it is a combination of hasty temper and a passionate reliance on quick judgments, which makes him rush to Delphi, then rush away from Delphi indignant with Apollo for not answering his question,[23] or jump to the conclusion that Jocasta's distress is caused by snobbery and anguish for having married a man who was not, after all, a king's son.[24] When he leaves Delphi, he is so sure of his assumptions that he does the two things he should never do: he kills a man who could well be his father, and marries a woman old enough to be his mother. Partly, he makes mistakes through the obsessions of a tyrant—that others are jealous and work through bribery and treachery to unseat him. This makes him assume, wrongly, that the outside brigands who killed Laius must have been suborned from inside Thebes,[25] and suspect that Polybus died through conspiracy.[26] It makes him break into the whole action against Creon and Tiresias. So far, he is the tragedy tyrant, like Creon in *Antigone* or Theseus in *Hippolytus*. But no farther. Oedipus condemns Creon without trial, but lets him off at the pleading of the Chorus, though he is sure they are wrong. And Oedipus can answer to the vague threats of Tiresias against him (443):

I do not care <what happens to me> if I save this city.

No tragedy tyrant could say that; and such a man is rewarded by the love and respect of his people (the Chorus)

---

[22] *Gnōmē.* See lines 393–98.
[23] Lines 785–97.
[24] Lines 1062–85.
[25] Line 124.
[26] Line 960.

such as no tragedy tyrant ever earns or gets.[27] Oedipus is a
tyrant, not *the* tyrant, and unique as he is, he is unique
again because he adds one more aspect: the lost child, the
strange, hunted creature who came from the mountain and
will go back to the mountain.

All combine in the most puzzling stasimon in *Oedipus*—
the second—after all has been called into question: the
honesty of Creon, the good sense of Oedipus, the official
report of the murder of Laius, the identity of the murderer,
the truth of oracles, the value of religion (863–910):

> May it be always given me to know
> guarded purity in all speech,
> in all action. For this, ordinances stand high
> in the bright mountain
> air where they were born. Olympus
> is their sole father. It was no
> mortal growth of men brought
> them forth: nor shall indifference
> store them away in sleep.
> Here the god stands great, ageless forever.
>
> Lust breeds the tyrant man. Lust,
> when fed and puffed with vanity
> on what disaccords with the time's advantage,
> clambering the sheer height
> goes over the drop, where nothing breaks his fall,
> where no firm foothold serves
> longer. But I pray god
> not to break that hand hold which serves
> well the community.
> I shall not loose my hold upon the god, my guide.
>
> But if one, gazing too high
> for thought and action, advances

---

[27] The outbursts at lines 660–64 and 689–96, spoken in the midst of
disagreement and disapproval, are among the most moving, certainly the
most moved and selfless, utterances of a Sophoclean Chorus I can find.

without fear of justice, without
caution, where spirits live,
may a bad fate seize him,
his wages for ill starred lusting,
if he gains unfairly his advantage,
nor refrains from the forbidden,
if he lays lewd hands on secret things.
What man shall hold off the bolts of god
from his life, in such action,
or if such works go unpunished, why
should I go through the ceremonies of worship?

No longer shall I go to the earth's
secret centerstone, religiously,
nor to the temple which is at Abae,
nor yet to Olympia,
no, unless this code is put together
to be manifest before mortals.
Then, oh Power, if Power is what you should be called,
Zeus, lord of all, oh give heed,
let your domain, ever immortal, not ignore.
For the old oracles for Laius are dying
out; men throw them aside
now, and nowhere is Apollo regarded.
God's worship is going.

To begin with the last: we are almost irresistibly forced
to think that this belongs to the time, about 426,[28] after
the death of Pericles and after the plague came out of
nowhere to waste Athens. Apollo had promised the Pelo-
ponnesians he would help them against Athens; the city
was full of oracles; the enlightened, one supposes, ignored
them. Apollo must show them. He showed them. He struck,
absurdly, unpredictably. The plague came. The failure of

[28] The play is usually dated shortly after 430; see Whitman, *Sophocles*,
pp. 49–50; 429 is often preferred, but it seems a little too close to the
plague, and 426 is slightly supported by Aristophanes *Acharnians* 27.

the intellectual, as of the tyrant, is to insist on his *own* *gnōmē*. Pericles was both intellectual and essentially tyrannical. But I go no further, for Oedipus was not Pericles. But his tragedy is the intellectual's tragedy: his tragic flaw, if you must, that his wit can not cover, foresee, account for all, and nonsensical forces can make nonsense of it; or, as Aeschylus put it, "Science is weaker than Nature is." [29]

Now to go back. The intellectual's tragedy is the tyrant's tragedy. "Lust breeds the tyrant man." Or is it "lust"? The word is *hybris*. Should we say "violence"? We have just emerged from the scene where Oedipus is most tyrannical. In the famous debate on forms of government in the third book of Herodotus, *hybris*, "lawless violence," marks the tyrant,[30] both the insane, bloody acts of Cambyses and the unscrupulous intrigues of Magian nobodies. *Hybris* combines with "jealousy" (*phthonos*) to make the tyrant suspicious of good men, vindictive, one who kills without due process of law, as Oedipus has just been saved from killing Creon.[31] Oedipus is too great to refuse his Chorus, but this is a personal favor; the almost crazy, uneasy suspicion remains.[32] But *hybris* not only characterizes the tyrant in action, it produces him; for escaping the violent tyrant, we may fall into the hands of the violent rabble or the violent nobles who by their violent disorder set up the situation for a redeemer and liberator—the tyrant again. Violence breeds the tyrant.

In a general sense. But we can get a still stricter meaning on another interpretation: the reference is to Jocasta and (it is only fair to add) Laius. The tragedy of incontinence: lust breeds (plants, begets) the tyrant. Against this, it can

---

[29] *Prometheus Bound* 530.
[30] Herodotus iii.80–82.
[31] Herodotus iii.80.5-*Oedipus* 623.
[32] Lines 658–59, 669–70.

be argued that the citizens (the Chorus) do not know that the child of Jocasta and Laius, who lusted and must breed, is now their tyrannical tyrant; they do not even think he is alive; and they and Jocasta have been working together in complete sympathy so that it would be strange for them to turn suddenly on her.

Yet I think it does apply to Jocasta,[33] since Sophocles fits the words to her, and the audience can pick up and follow. Like Oedipus again and again through the ironies of the play, the Chorus say more than they know. All meanings are combined: the civic violence which breeds the tyrant, the tyrant's violence which makes him tyrannical in action, with the violence of lust breeding the tyrant, the child who should never have been born [34] and who, born in defiance, lays hands on secret places and defiles his mother,[35] the wife who is no wife.[36]

Along with this, we have the persistent imagery of the climber on the mountain, in high places where spirits live and the overdrop is sheer, danger natural and supernatural, where the climber must use not only feet but hands, and

[33] At line 719, Jocasta says that Laius cast out the infant "by the hands of others"; at lines 1171–74, the Theban Shepherd says that Jocasta gave him the infant. Lapse by Sophocles (conceivable) or intention?

[34] On the birth of Pisistratus, tyrant of Athens, see Herodotus i.59.1–3. In regard to a portent, Chilon the Spartan, a wise man in general and in particular an anti-tyrant, warned Hippocrates against rearing a son, but Hippocrates would not obey him. See also Herodotus v.92β–δ for the story of the birth of the predestined tyrant-child Cypselus, the emissaries sent to kill him, and the concealment of the child by his mother. In the lost *Oedipus* of Carcinus (Nauck, p. 798) Jocasta put off the man who was trying to find her son. This may mean that Carcinus followed a version which combined the foundling-theme with the outline of a dynastic drama, for which indeed the Oedipus legend contained the materials; see Robert, *Oidipus*, pp. 305–11.

[35] Hippias the tyrant, son of Pisistratus, dreamed that he lay with his mother, Herodotus vi.107.1. See Sophocles *Oedipus* 980–82. My translation of line 891 is influenced by Sophocles' *The Women of Trachis* 565.

[36] Line 1256.

needs a guide—ideally a divine guide.[37] No recorded Greek ever climbed a mountain for the sport of mountain-climbing, and the notion of finding the hardest way up a peak is peculiarly gothic or baroque for an Athenian, or, as Spengler would say, Faustian; but there were occasions, religious and military occasions at least, when mountains had to be climbed. The mountain-climb figured early, from Hesiod on, as a symbol of the slippery, punishing, dangerous quest for achievement or excellence (*aretē*) which stood at the top; [38] just as, in this stasimon, the laws of righteousness stand in the thin, pure Olympian air.

The Greek wilderness is the mountains. All cultures have their wildernesses. The northern foundling might be a child of the great forest, but Greece is not a land of flat forests; its wilderness, whether of woods or scrubby barrens or cliff and boulder, is of the big mountains which are scarcely ever out of sight anywhere in mainland Greece.[39] These were the domain of emptiness, spirits, wild beasts, and tough shepherds; the Athenian city man knew little of them, not that he did not lead a hardy life of military service that would seem impossibly strenuous today, but the citizen-spearman was a fighter of the plains and more at home on a warship than on a mountain top.[40]

[37] While I cannot exclude the idea of a mountain climber from my mind, I am far from claiming that this is the sole and all-sufficient clue to the passage. All the key terms have multiple meanings. At line 876 Wolff's γεῖσ' ἀναβᾶσ' for εἰσαναβᾶσ', adopted also by Pearson, (see his Apparatus) is most seductive (a *snow*-cornice such as I have met on Parnassus) but ought to be resisted.

[38] Hesiod's *Works and Days* 287–92, the original steep and thorny way opposed to the primrose path; Simonides, frg. 37 (Diehl); Pindar *Ol.* 9.107–108, with scholia. For Prodicus' fable of Heracles at the crossroads see Xenophon *Memorabilia* ii.20–34, where the Hesiodic passage is also quoted, but the image of the difficult way is not concretely developed.

[39] See Carpenter, *Folk Tale, Fiction, and Saga in the Homeric Epics*, pp. 18–20.

[40] For the discomfiture of Lacedaemonian hoplites in rough, precipitous

The mountains were the wilderness, and for Thebes in particular, *the* mountain was Cithaeron, a bold black trapezoid dominating the Asopus Valley. Parnassus is higher, steeper, and snowier, but a sacred mountain with civilized Delphi perched in its underslopes. Cithaeron is all wild.

On such mountain sides the Chorus imagine the outcast murderer (463–82):

> Who is he, whom the magic-singing
> Delphian rock proclaimed
> the bloody-handed murderer
> whose crimes were too deep to tell?
> Run, he must run now
> harder than stormy horses,
> feet flying in flight,
> for the armed god is after him, leaping
> with fire and flash, Apollo, Zeus' own,
> and the forbidding Death-
> Spirits horribly haunt him.
>
> The message shone, it showed
> even now from the snows
> of Parnassus. Manhunt the hidden
> man. After him all.
> He lurks, a wild bull
> in the wild wood, in the holes
> of the rock side
> lonely-footed, forlorn wandering,
> dodging aside from the mid-centered
> prophecies, which, things alive,
> hover to haunt him.

In the first long angry response of Tiresias, where the chief image is of a ship come home to harbor (obvious enough),

country, see Thucydides iv.29–38; of Athenian hoplites caught in a mountain defile, Thucydides iii.95–98.

the mountain, and the stalker on the mountain, project,
even obtrude (412–23):

I tell you, since you have baited me with my blindness:
you have your eyes, and do not see where you are standing
in evil, nor where you are living, nor whom you are living with.
Do you know whose son you are? Unconscious enemy
of your own people, here on earth, and under the ground,
the double-goading curse, father's and mother's in one,
shall stalk you on its feet of horror from this land,
you who see straight now, but shall then see only dark.
What harbor shall not be full of your cries,
what Mount Cithaeron shall not echo to them soon
when you learn what that marriage is, that awful haven
where, after your fair voyage, you brought in your ship?

The foundling, in Greece, was the child of the mountain
side. The foundling was often protected by divine wild
spirits of the place, or he might have been a spirit himself,
or even a great god, Dionysus, Hermes, even Zeus.[41] The
Chorus fancy Oedipus, the mountain-child, fosterling of
Cithaeron, as by-blow of some mountain-walking god, Pan,
Apollo, Hermes, or Dionysus, by one of the nymphs of the
mountains.[42] Oedipus, in answer to the doubts, as he thinks,
of Jocasta, identifies himself with nature (1076–85):

Let her break forth her tempers as she will, but I
will still find out what seed made me, although it be
humble. She being proud, perhaps, as women are,
thinks the obscurity of my birth is some disgrace.
I count myself the child of Fortune. While her gifts
are good, I shall not call myself degraded. I
am born of her. She is my mother. And the months
my brothers marked me small, and they have marked me great.
So born, I would not ever wish I had been born
anything else, to keep me from learning who I am.

[41] See Harrison, *Themis*, pp. 1–49.
[42] Lines 1098–1109.

Tychē, Fortune or Coincidence, is here the way in which things come out or work, that is, another Greek way of saying Nature. The natural son is the child of Nature. After the catastrophe, it is to nature and the pathos of places that Oedipus chiefly appeals (1391–1403):

> Cithaeron oh Cithaeron, why did you take me? Why
> did you not kill me when you took me? Thus had I
> never made clear to men the place where I was born.
> O Polybus and Corinth and my father's house
> of old, as men then called it, what a festering sore
> you fed beneath my outward splendor, I who now
> have been found evil in myself, and evil born.
> O three roads, hidden valley,
> oak wood and narrow meeting at the threeway cross,
> who drank the blood of my own father which was spilled
> by my own hands, do you remember still
> what things I did to you, and then, when I came here,
> what things I did again?

It is as if Oedipus had been set free from ordinary city life when he was put away into the hands of the mountain Shepherd. It is natural that the child of the wilderness who lived in the city should go home to his wilderness to die— to ask to go, even though the story has not told that he did so; and thus we have come back to our beginning (1449–54):

> But let it never be thought right that I should stay
> in the city of my father, and be part of it,
> but let me go to the mountains and live there, where stands
> Cithaeron, called *my* mountain, which, when they still lived
> my mother and my father gave me, for my final tomb.
> So let them kill me at last, for they destroyed my life.

We have completed the circle but we have not resolved all the play. Never think that. We can read *Oedipus* as many times as we like, and every time find new truths and throw away old falsehoods that once seemed to be true. There is always a dimension that escapes.

While it is true that *Oedipus* is a particularly compact combination of themes, where themes of foundling, mountain-spirit, murder, manhunt, tyrant cohere because we are constantly led from one into the other, yet in this play one can, perhaps more clearly than elsewhere in Sophocles, separate the poetic from the dramatic. Or at least we can separate the "daemonic" or "barbaric," because it is not absolutely needed. There are splendid characterizing lines and rhetorical effects, without this kind of poetic material. And the daemonic is not "so." The finished play is not about any nature-child or mountain-spirit. He exists only in the imagination of the players. The Oedipus of the action is a perfectly plausible, too human man, and the closest he has ever come to being a child of Fortune or Nature, or Year Spirit with the months for brothers, is to be handed from one kindhearted Shepherd to another, in a summer of babyhood on the high pastures. The play King, with his greatnesses and his faults, does not need to be a splendid barbarian at heart, like Ajax. He is a homicide: but on the level of discourse we may see him as thinking himself so set upon, so right in his defense, that the deadly brawl at the crossroads has scarcely troubled his conscience since. He never was a hunted monster, something like a great, wild beast, fierce but scary, driven among the high rocks. That is all the imagination of old men. We can so play trenchant characters that all seems motivated, and we can forget that what first drove the action was the shape of a universal pattern story from the childhood of men.

Oedipus is acted today, often professionally, and more frequently, I believe, than any other Greek play. It is commonly given in what almost passes as an authorized version

—that of Yeats—which has cut down or cut out those daemonic passages we have been considering.[43] It is good theatre, and it is truly dramatic, but it is no longer haunted.

In a stasimon of *Antigone*,[44] also, among the moralities we see an image of the high snows of Olympus where Zeus is forever, deathless and sleepless, with his laws; and by contrast, an image of the pit below, this time the darkness of the sea stirred to waves that batter the promontories. The gods of Sophocles are there, but remote, unattainable as the snows of Olympus; we can only see the effects, and are closer to the dark underpit. The tragedies of Sophocles concern resolute, intelligent, civilized people, determined to understand everything; they never do, because there is a dark nonsensical element in things, which eludes their comprehension and, often, destroys them; but which has its own wild beauty.

[43] See above, note 3.
[44] Lines 582–625.

V

EURIPIDES

Medea

Helen

᚛᚛᚛᚛᚛᚛᚛᚛᚛᚛᚛᚛᚛᚛᚛᚛᚛᚛᚛᚛᚛᚛᚛

EURIPIDES was born about 480 B.C. and died
in 407 or 406. He was thus at least fifteen years younger
than Sophocles and died a year or so earlier. His first dramatic presentation is dated 455 B.C. Aeschylus had just died,
and Sophocles was the acknowledged master of Athenian
theatre. At that time, there was perhaps little for an am-
bitious Athenian poet to make a career of except his own
version of Sophoclean tragedy. Epic belonged to another
age; elegy, which Greek men of letters turned out as naturally as Elizabethan men of letters turned out sonnets, remained a private and minor medium; comedy, that is,
Attic Old Comedy, one may say flatly, was not for a man
like Euripides; and choral lyric in the grand manner, still
being practiced by Pindar and Bacchylides, had in Athens

103

been channeled into the scheme of tragedy. In this specially Athenian form, the young poet practically was forced to follow the lead of Aeschylus, or of Sophocles, and here again I think there was not much choice. In 455 the *Oresteia*, Aeschylus' greatest, was only three years gone, but nothing would have been more evident than that this magnificent combination of dramatic naïveté and enduring modernity in lyrical imagery belonged to the old master and could not be re-created, certainly not by a man in his twenties just beginning. The Sophoclean form, of single tragedy, with actors and iambic dominant over chorus and lyric, and invaded by the spirit of sophistic debate, was the form dictated to a modern or progressive poet. In another age, Euripides might, like Hardy or Meredith, have combined the careers of novelist and lyric poet, with high ambitions toward both forms, but in fifth-century Athens the novel did not exist, and the stride was far too great for the age. Euripides was saddled with Sophocles. For dramatic competition, Sophocles was "there."

Nor did Euripides ever catch up with him. He won only five firsts in tragic competition, and one of these was posthumous. He was mercilessly parodied by the comic poets. We may think now that Aristophanes' *Frogs* is, in truth, a great tribute, and that Aristophanes found him much more interesting than he found Sophocles; but the *Frogs* came after Euripides died—he could scarcely have appreciated it anyway—and the attacks of the comedians were not likely to have sweetened his life. He found himself more and more out of sympathy with the policies of his once-beloved Athens, and at last left it for good and died in Macedonia.[1] His failures and defeats left unmistakable marks on his work.

[1] For biographical details, see Schmid, *Geschichte der griechischen Literatur*, III, 313–28.

This approach, though valid, is negative. Euripides worked in a medium which was not of his own invention, or altogether of his own choice, but he made it his own.

With Euripides, drama moves another step toward realism. Sophocles said that he made men as they ought to be, or as one ought to make them, but Euripides made men as they are.[2] This shows in various ways. Sophocles projected an illusion of reality in his powerful characters, who yet are not full portraits of flesh and blood people but only characterized in those salients which adapt them to the ceremonies of the Sophoclean action. Euripides scrutinized the persons of heroic legend to see how he might make them act their stories in the likeness of men and women we might know in his day or ours. His Admetus is a spoiled rich boy, Clytemestra an agreeable snob, Hermione a disagreeable snob, Orestes a manic-depressive, Achilles an Ivy League athlete, Jason a down-at-the-heel aristocrat turned social climber. He exploits such unheroic motives as irritation, frustration, exasperation, the impertinence of servants, the cattiness of women in the presence of superior beauty (or of men in the presence of superior strength), the purely social embarrassment of the upper middle classes caught in awkward situations. He brings tragedy into the home and the park and the house around the corner, where "the wife talked, and the servant talked, the master, the maid, and the granny." [3] But this was not all he did, for he did not succeed in going all the way toward prose drama or prosaic drama; his plays are not mimes; he did not break away from the high tragical line, neither the sublimities nor the fustians of his predecessors, and he used divine appearances, miraculous transportations through space, dragon chariots, paraphernalia of the supernatural which sometimes sort

[2] See above, chapter 3, note 15.
[3] Aristophanes' *Frogs* 949–50.

most oddly with the direction and tone of the underlying theme. For his eye and his hand did wander, and sometimes his attention was diverted from poetry and action to some point or issue he would rather establish than make his play a thing of perfection.

For such external reasons, but for reasons from inside also, the incipient realistic play is not always a complete success. Let us consider one drama which at least has strong moments, *Medea*. Here, it has been said, we see inside the soul of a woman as no Greek writer ever made us see before.[4] And this is entirely true; but the analysis exacts its price. The high horror of the action comes when Medea kills her children. Why does she kill them? We are given, not one compelling motive but a whole assortment of motives. She kills them because she hates them, because she loves them, to spite and hurt Jason, to leave him without posterity, to vindicate the rights and prestige of herself and her country, to save them from the Corinthians who, she supposes, would kill them if she did not. In the end she does not know why she kills them and neither do we. But, we have said, we ought perhaps not to think too much about rational or psychological motivation, but only the inevitable sequences of action. We can think of several reasons why Oedipus should blind himself, but these too-many reasons do not stunt the force of his act. That is because the act is self-expressive and motives come as afterthoughts. Medea acts, or is supposed to act, on sheer drive of feeling, irrational or barbaric or simply female. But we do not feel the drive, because the motives are constantly being forced on our attention. Instead of striding forward with irresistible momentum, Medea keeps getting stuck and having to lash herself along. And here is the insincerity. From the outset, in the text and not in our imagina-

[4] Pohlenz, *Die griechische Tragödie*, p. 258.

tion, we are given a woman who enrages herself. "There," says the nurse, "children, do you hear? Your mother stirs up her heart, stirs up her gall." Or, again, "she will kindle the stormcloud of her sorrow with growing anger." [5] By the time she reaches the great monologue in which she harangues herself forward toward her acts, self-flagellation has involved self-dramatization too. I cannot help feeling that, by this time, Medea, who is practiced in deceit of others, is putting on an act for her own benefit, that the mother-love is phony and that Jason, cold and smug though he may be, loves the children better than Medea does. All this is horribly natural. This is what people are like— Medea is truer to life than Antigone or Ajax—but the pace and force of action in dramatic illusion have been sacrificed. The gain is naturalistic detail.

Probably the sacrifice was unintentional. A part of the dramatic confusion comes from the very unwillingness of Euripides to sacrifice anything. Medea is a realistic drama, which might perhaps have been happier in prose, uneasily mounted on the frame of heroic legend and the verse schemes of antique tragedy. The heroine might have been treated as a forsaken foreign wife (this is the dominant concept) or as any forsaken wife not necessarily barbarian, or as a potent and almost superhuman end-of-the-world witch, or even a minor goddess. Euripides sees her principally as the forsaken foreign wife, but momentarily in all the other concepts too. Thus, for instance, Medea, before embarking on her murders, has arranged with her friend Aegeus, king of Athens, to take refuge with him; but she must find her own way to Athens.[6] She acts here as the wronged, conspiratorial woman, and she needs some realistic intrigue for escape from Corinth. But at the end of the

[5] *Medea* 98–99, 107–108; see also, line 157.
[6] Lines 709–30.

play, as Jason beats on the doors, Medea appears sky-borne in a chariot drawn by dragons, like a Thetis or Artemis or Athene to found the cult and predict the future, like an immortal goddess revealed in splendor—and then announces that she is taking that chariot to Athens where she means to settle down. One thing or the other, we might say; make up your mind; either Medea is a wronged, revengeful wife making a planned getaway, in which case we want a cloak and a hood and a small boat, or she is the goddess who married a mortal, like Thetis, whose story hers could almost be,[7] saying farewell and departing from actuality to the end of the earth, to the Ocean, or clean out of our human world, back where she came from and where she belongs. Then the dragon chariot would be appropriate. When it is used as a taxi to get from Corinth to Athens, it is preposterous. The real trouble, perhaps, is that the spectacular supernatural is used not simply to flourish an epilogue, as in *Electra*, but to solve the problems of an action which has, hitherto, moved on the plane of human experience within natural laws.

Medea, despite all these faults, is a potent play because of its arresting situation with which we start, its fine writ-

[7] See the list of goddesses who mated with mortal men in Hesiod's *Theogony* 965–1020. There Medea appears (992–1002, not named, but described as the daughter of Aeëtes) along with Thetis, Harmonia, Eos, etc. Her son Medeius was, like Thetis' Achilles, reared on the mountain by Chiron (1000–1002). According to the author of the early *Aegimius*, Thetis tried to immortalize her children by boiling them; see H. G. Evelyn-White, *Hesiod* (3rd. ed., London, 1936), p. 273. Medea, a pre-eminent cutter-up and boiler-woman, may well thus have killed her children in the original story; see Page, Introduction to *Medea*, pp. xxi–xxiii. In our play, Medea the witch-woman promises to rejuvenate Aegeus, 717–18; compare the promise of Thetis to Peleus in Euripides' *Andromache* 1253–62, very different indeed, but perhaps developed from a similar legend-pattern. Both Thetis and Medea won the favor of Hera by refusing Zeus. See Page, *loc. cit.*, and, for all details, see Preller-Robert, ii, 65–80 (Thetis), 185–89 (Medea).

ing in detail, and its simply beating us over the head with horror and pity for Medea's victims. But we can see the beginning of the fragmentation of tragedy, and can imagine how after a generation or so of this there may well be no tragedy left.

Euripides' version of Electra may be compared with those of Aeschylus and Sophocles, since all three have survived. Euripides seems to have set out to show how this story could have been enacted, plausibly and believably, and by people we might know; and he has been uncommonly successful. We can start anywhere and deduce the rest of the main features. For instance, how does a hero who returns from exile without armed force manage to kill an established tyrant? How does he cope with the palace guard? Answer: he does not go near the city or the palace. He sets on Aegisthus in the country, where the tyrant is sacrificing and off guard, and his escort are mere armed slaves who can be cowed or persuaded, and Clytemestra has been diverted to the country dwelling of Electra, who pretends she has had a baby. With these ends, there necessarily cohere the marriage of Electra to a farmer and the Chorus of country girls. It is natural to find Orestes skulking about the extreme borders of Argive territory because he has failed to make up his mind to the necessary murders and is not even sure he wants to be recognized by his sister. The gruesome, frantic, half-botched slaughter of Aegisthus by a terrified assassin slashing with a meat cleaver, the slaughter of Clytemestra by the same assassin, still scared and prodded by his sister, the rather likable villains, the self-dramatizing sister, the nervous brother—all the elements are artistically combined to produce a stupid, vicious muddle which is so horribly natural that we do say: "This is what it could really have been like." Almost, at least. The high tragical language at times goes oddly in a drama which should have been in prose, where such poetry as there is has little to do with the action and is there because of the requirements of dramatic structure, and for relief.

Relief and escape are the counter-themes to Euripides' naturalism. When (in *Hippolytus*) Phaedra is caught in the entanglement which is the consequence of her own irresolution, and goes, with words of ill omen, back into the house, the Chorus of Troezenian women sing the ode that serves as a curtain between acts. They are an ideal-spectator Chorus, sympathetic but not involved, and there is no reason why they should not go on leading happy lives, but they sing of escape, and the longing for escape, to caves in the sea cliffs where the birds make their nests, and over the sea to the end of the Adriatic where Phaethon's sisters weep for him and their tears are drops of amber under the water. This is the theme of the play, one of the escapist's tragedies by the writer who was never easy in his own context, whether literary or material. Again and again, his players, like their poet, wish that the world were not what it is, or that they could go, as they cannot, to some delightful elsewhere, there or there or there. They wish, where Sophoclean people will.

Euripides swings back and forth between these themes. It is the escapist who sentimentalizes the underprivileged and downtrodden, children, women, slaves, prisoners, barbarians, but it is the realist who sees the counter-theme to learning through suffering, that brutality brutalizes, that we may weep for poor Alcmene or Hecuba, but if they ever get into position to hit back, we had better run for our lives, because they will be deadlier than their oppressors ever were.[8]

The tendency is toward the fragmentation of tragedy,

[8] See Dodds, Introduction to *Euripides: Bacchae*, p. xliii.

both in the separation of issues and arguments from dramatic themes, and in the separation of the nonpoetic from the poetic. Prose drama with lyric interludes might, we think, have served him. But as a matter of fact, it did not. He wrote verse plays, as did his contemporaries.[9] What, then, of the poetry, how did he use it, and to what effect?

First, in simplest terms, if a poet writes plays in verse, that verse may be in itself advantageous or disadvantageous to the play by being, as verse, good, bad, or indifferent. We could have made our whole study of the poetry of Greek tragedy from this commonsense point of view. It would, through translations, have been dull. But, since Euripides is in craftsmanship and quality more variable than Aeschylus or Sophocles, let me briefly sample and illustrate, if I can, his good verse and his less good verse.

In *Alcestis*, the heroine has died for the sake of her husband and has been taken away to the place of burial. Now Admetus has come back, has seen that he ought not have let her die,[10] and has seen what the rest of his life will be. The Chorus attempt to console him. In *The Children of Heracles*, the cause of the children of Heracles and their protectors, the Athenians, has demanded a human sacrifice, and Macaria, daughter of Heracles, has volunteered and

[9] On the development of the realistic prose mime, see A. Körte, in Pauly-Wissowa, *R.E.*, s.v. "Sophron." The latter, beloved and perhaps adapted by Plato, was probably a contemporary of Euripides. There was, in Euripides' time, no public career as a mime-writer open to an Athenian.

[10] A. M. Dale denies this, Introduction to *Euripides: Alcestis*, pp. xxiv–xxv: "The bitter lesson Admetus learns in his ἄρτι μανθάνω is not 'I see now that I ought never to have accepted this sacrifice', but 'I see now that Alcestis in dying is better off than I in living, since I have lost my happiness and my reputation'." But I think Miss Dale has pushed a good argument too far. "He hates his parents, but was unwilling to die himself" (lines 958–59); what can this mean except that he, at least, should not have wanted Alcestis to die in his place?

gone to her death, despite the remonstrances of Iolaus.
The Chorus attempt to console him and the survivors. I
give both odes, first *Alcestis* (962–1007):

I myself, in the transports
of mystic verses, as in study
of history and science, have found
nothing so strong as Compulsion,
nor any means to combat her,
not in the Thracian books set down
in verse by the school of Orpheus,
not in all the remedies Phoebus has given the heirs
of Asclepius to fight the many afflictions of man.

She alone is a goddess
without altar or image to pray
before. She heeds no sacrifice.
Majesty, bear no harder
on me than you have in my life before!
All Zeus even ordains
only with you is accomplished.
By strength you fold and crumple the steel of the Chalybes.
There is no pity in the sheer barrier of your will.

Now she has caught your wife in the breakless grip of her hands.
Take it. You will never bring back, by crying,
the dead into the light again.
Even the sons of the gods fade
and go in death's shadow.
She was loved when she was with us.
She shall be loved still, now she is dead.
It was the best of all women to whom you were joined in
    marriage.

The monument of your wife must not be counted among the
    graves
of the dead, but it must be given its honors
as gods are, worship of wayfarers.

And as they turn the bend of the road
and see it, men shall say:
"She died for the sake of her husband.
Now she is a blessed spirit.
Hail, majesty, be gracious to us." Thus will men speak in her
    presence.

Then *The Children of Heracles* (608–29):

I say that without the gods no man is blissful, no man is
    crushed with adversity,
nor can the same house stand firm in fortune
for all time. Fate drives it
variously. She
makes brief the stay of one who lives on the heights,
but raises to prosperity the poor vagabond.
What is foredoomed we have no right to shun, no
man by intelligence can push it aside, and he who tries
shall have spent labor and no profit.

Though you have been cast down, take what the gods give nor
with pain overgrieve your mind.
She, who died so pitiful for her brothers
and country has her portion of honor in death.
Not without glory
shall be her reputation left among men.
Courage strides on firm through affliction.
Worthy is what she has done, of her father,
of her high birth. Yet, if you must grieve for the death
of the brave, I must grieve with you.

    In thought and meaning the odes are quite similar. I find
the *Alcestis* ode immeasurably superior, both in Greek and
in my translation. The one from *The Children of Heracles*
has no palpable faults of wandering attention, bad taste,
shoddy prosody; it seems merely flat, abstract, and unorigi-
nal, as if Euripides were going through familiar motions.
The *Alcestis* ode contrasts the figure of compulsion,

Anangkē, Nature as law—the simple fact that people die—
a goddess unworshiped because there is no use worshiping
her, against the worshiped woman, Alcestis the Saint in her
wayside shrine. But Macaria could have her cult too.[11]
Euripides is not much interested in her. Just before this
ode, she makes her farewell in a series of end-stopped
iambic sentences, disposing of her case point by point just
where we expect her to take off and run free, removing herself from the drama in which her appearance is only an
episode. Alcestis, in her farewell speech, is chilly toward
Admetus but is carried on an undercurrent of strong feeling, and her iambic lines run over, move, and flow.

Iambics, better and worse, may be compared in two short
scenes with almost identical structure from *Hippolytus* and
Andromache. Theseus believed his son, Hippolytus, had
forced Phaedra to suicide. He called the curse of Poseidon
against him and sent him out of the land. Peleus, on the
other hand, had heard of a plot in Delphi against Neoptolemus, his grandson, and was alarmed. The two scenes intro-
duce the Messenger, who will go on to recount the catastrophe, the death of the young hero. First *Hippolytus*
(1157–72):

Theseus, the story I have to tell should trouble you,
and your people, those who live in the city of Athens
and those also of the Troezenian district.

What is your story? Has some disaster fallen
upon our two neighboring cities?

Hippolytus is gone. So I can say. He sees
the sunlight still, but his strength is faint, and going.

Who did it? Surely, someone he had quarreled with,
whose wife he forced and shamed, as he did his father's?

[11] See W. Schirmer, in Roscher's *Lexikon*, ii, col. 2291, s.v. "Makaria."

His own chariot horses destroyed him. They
and the curses of your mouth with which you called
the ruler of the sea, your father, against your son.

O gods. Poseidon, you were shown in truth to be
my father, for you listened when I prayed to you.
How did he perish? Speak. How did the trap of Justice
spring its beam to strike him, who disgraced me?

Now *Andromache* (1070–84):

Ah me.
What news it is my wretched errand to announce,
what news for you, old sir, and all my master's friends.

Ah, my mind, as if prophetic, is full of dread.

Your grandson, most revered Peleus, is gone.
This you must know. The cause was sword strokes given him
by the men of Delphi and the Mycenaean stranger.
Take care, old sir. What are you doing. Do not fall.
Lift yourself up.

                    No, I am done. I am destroyed.
My voice is gone. My feet have no strength to bear me up.

But lift yourself and hear me tell you what the event
has been. You must, if you would help your friends at all.

O my fate, how wretchedly you have befallen me
here in old age and at the very bourne of life.
The one son of my only son. How did he go?
Disclose. I do not want to hear it, but must hear.

This again is not positively bad, but mediocre, which is
worse than bad. The situation is a stock situation; the expedient of making the poor old man fall down or almost
fall down adds only melodrama. Anyone who could manage iambic lines at all could write as well as this. But perhaps the underlying cause of mediocrity is the fact that, in

this play, we have never met Neoptolemus and cannot be very much interested in him. The lines from *Hippolytus* are excellent, not because of their special imagery or rhetoric, but because they are adequate to the drama, which is a beautiful action. The situation is not a stock situation; the resentment of Theseus against Hippolytus is soberly counterplayed with the resentment of the Messenger against Theseus.

To flatness, which seems the exaggeration of sheer indifference, we can oppose overelaboration and fussiness and fustian. If the former belongs specially to Euripides, this last is a disfigurement endemic in poetical tragedy from Aeschylus to Shakespeare and his successors. But Euripides has special faults of this sort. Unlike Aeschylus and Sophocles, he is given to the sentimental repeat, as in *Helen* (194–95; 213–16):

> from Achaea a mariner
> came, yes came, and tears on my tears he loaded

countermatched by

> a life. better unlived
> given to you, yes given, when Zeus blazed in the bright
> air, in the snowflash of the swan's
> wing to beget you upon your mother,

where the limpid vision is a little spoiled by the fretful prettiness that introduces it. A fine instance of the pretty style comes from the Phrygian eunuch's solo in *Orestes* (1426–30):

> It chanced that with Phrygian, Phrygian motions
> I fanned the breeze, the breeze, on the curls
> of Helen, yes of Helen, with a pretty
> feathered fan, yes with a fan I fanned her cheek
> in sweeping and exotic motions.

But the faults of this manner, if faults at all, are faults of original taste and choice, not execution. The melody that must have gone with these flights may have improved them (it may also have made them worse).[12] In *Orestes*, Euripides certainly knew what he was about; it may even be that he was his own best parodist.

To sum up: the verse of Euripidean tragedy contains good verse and bad verse. We can say, and we could to some extent show in detail, that his most nearly perfect plays, *Alcestis*, *Helen*, *Hippolytus*, *The Bacchae*, especially the last two, are well versified throughout; that his poorer plays, *The Children of Heracles*, *Andromache*, *The Suppliant Women*, *The Phoenician Maidens* have much indifferent or poor versification. Is it simply that poetry which is adequate to an otherwise good play is good poetry, or can we find, as we have for Aeschylus and Sophocles, some special, arbitrary sense in which the poetry as poetry can be more than adequate, and give an extra dimension to the tragedy?

One of the most familiar and identifiable uses of poetry in Euripides is for contrast and relief. The theme of escape is in every play, like other relief themes most easily found in choral passages but by no means confined to them. If only I could go away, the Chorus sing in *The Bacchae*,[13] to Paphos on Cyprus, island of Aphrodite and the Love-Cherubs, or to Pieria and the slopes of Olympus haunted by the Muses, the Graces, and all sweetness (*pothos*). The Chorus of *Hippolytus*,[14] we have seen, long for caves in the sea cliffs or far waters and shores, to be free to wander

[12] There is evidence for a coloratura manner of delivery in Aristophanes' *Frogs* 1348, in the midst of a sublime takeoff on the Euripidean monody, 1331–63.

[13] Lines 402–15.

[14] Lines 732–51.

like birds. In *Helen*,[15] the exiled Greek women think of the Sidonian galley sweeping toward Greece across quiet waters blessed by Galatea, nymph of calms, the green daughter of the great Sea, but they, too, drift into the wish to join the migrant birds, cranes or geese, who cross and recross between Africa and Europe. The thought of escape, under ground or into the sky, becomes half formulaic. In *Hippolytus*, Artemis apparently speaks to Theseus in his grief and guilt (1290–95):

> How can you keep from hiding yourself
> and your shame in the caverned deeps of the earth
> or skyward on wings
> lift yourself clear of this life, its sorrow,
> since among good men life holds for you
> no part any more?

In *Heracles*, the hero who has murdered his family in a fit of madness demands (1157–58):

How can I take wings, or plunge deep under ground, to find some place that is desolate of evil things? [16]

Contrast and relief come in with their lyric dimension in other ways than by the impossible wish or the optatives of desired escape. Medea has horrified her friends and trusted confidantes, the women of Corinth, by announcing her plan to murder her children, having now arranged to go to Athens; but how can such a woman be received and live among the Athenians? For theirs is a city happy and favored by the gods from time primeval, never stormed in war, full of wisdom and art and love, blessed with bright air and temperate winds and health, and in all things complete.[17] The picture may be idealized; it lends a little desired sweet-

---

[15] Lines 1451–86.
[16] Compare *Ion* 1238–43.
[17] *Medea* 823–50.

ness to a play which will get none from any of its characters. Euripides plays his scenes of calm order against the brutalities and the nasty intrigues of his actions. Hippolytus, sentimental and self-satisfied over his favoring goddess, can enjoy his green, unspoiled meadow and his wreath for a moment before he is shocked, smeared, and killed. *Ion* opens with that unpretentious young man pottering blissfully about the front of the temple, armed with a bow (to scare away the birds) and a sprig of laurel (which is a broom and which he addresses as if it were Mr. Wilkinson's spade) and a watering pot—and lyric song. He is, in fact, Apollo's janitor, or should one say verger? He is Apollo's son, too, and will learn this, and, unlike Hippolytus, he will survive his play and go on to glory, but he will never again be so happy. Euripides had an eye that could see the essential grace in workaday groups: hence, his choral entrances of *Hippolytus* and *Helen* with their "I was just out washing the clothes and spreading them on the rocks to dry." To the picturesqueness of such groups described is added their suitability to the grapevine of gossip, good motivation for bringing a group of women onto the stage. Against the frigid unpleasantness of the action in *Andromache* is placed a rather appetizing impression of the goddesses appearing before Paris to be judged.[18] We escape from *Electra* to a vision of dolphins in the spray at the ship's prow and the water full of Nereids.[19] In the imagination of elsewhere, Euripides seems sometimes to have recovered and exploited the special manner of Aeschylus—but with a difference: the stately pageant is gone, action, usually, is relieved rather than enlarged, and the mood has become wistful.

Thus far, we have dealt with relief themes as they occur, piecemeal. For some tragedies, however, it is possible, with-

[18] Lines 279–92.
[19] Lines 432–51.

out strain on the material, to see the poetry as the persistent expression of ideas which characterize and generate the action of the play. I find such poetry, which might be called thematic, in *Hippolytus, Alcestis, Iphigenia in Tauris, The Trojan Women, Helen,* and *The Bacchae.* The idea of love, guilty or innocent, profane or sacred, dominates the story of *Hippolytus.* However we may put this in terms of theology or ethics, the fact is there, and bursts out in all choral passages and many of the spoken lines. *Alcestis* is more complex. It seems to deal with human beings faced with the facts of existence and death, the laws of Nature, named here as *Anangkē* or Compulsion, featureless, unpersonified, not worth praying to because there is no divine entity to receive the prayer, only blank force (the miracle and the restoration are a notional favor of one god, not earned and never to be repeated). Consequently, the poetry deals always with those themes that the Greeks voiced when death did come to them: the contrast with former happiness, and the consolations in the community of death, memory, glory, and tomb cult. *Iphigenia in Tauris* is the story of desperate Greeks in Barbary and their escape toward home, and homesickness is the dominant, or at least a dominant, theme of the play.

In 415 B.C., after Athens had captured and destroyed the neutral island state of Melos, and on the eve of the great Athenian expedition against Sicily, Euripides presented a trilogy with satyr-play on related themes, all dealing with the tale of Troy. The tragedies were, in order, *Alexander, Palamedes, The Trojan Women,* and *Sisyphus.* All but *The Trojan Women* are lost. *Alexander,* the story of the prophecies concerning the infant Alexander (Paris), his exposure, preservation, and ultimate return and recognition, ironically led off with what was in itself the happy found-ling–romance—of the glorious man who destroyed his city.

Palamedes was the story of the wise man in the state, undone by the jealousy of unscrupulous politicians. Odysseus must have been the chief villain here. In *The Trojan Women* he is the ruthless counselor behind the scenes, author of the worst brutalities committed by the victorious Achaeans. The satyr-play may well have recounted the disreputable begetting or birth of this character.[20]

In *The Trojan Women* the city has been taken, and the men destroyed; the captive women are being dealt out to their new masters. There is little action, rather a string of episodes until the eldest and greatest of the Troades, Troy herself, crashes in flames before our eyes. What holds the drama together is a set of related themes, voiced in the choral odes and in the speeches as well. This Troy, seen mangled and defiled, had once been a happy, human place to live in.[21] The gods particularly had loved it; now they have given it to the brutal soldiers, while immortal Trojans, Ganymede and Tithonus, taken up among the gods and made a part of the Olympian company, move among the Olympians in the sky, remotely smiling and heedless of the destruction of their city and their people.

> For the gods loved Troy once.
> Now they have forgotten.[22]

If any community had seemed impregnable once, it was Troy with her walls. If any army seems invincible now, it is the Greek with its ships. Walls and ships are their respective emblems throughout the play. The walls have been

---

[20] This is only a guess from the title. But the story that Odysseus was the bastard son of Sisyphus, who seduced Anticlea, goes with anti-Odyssean sentiments to be found in Attic tragedy, e.g., Aeschylus frg. 175, Nauck; Sophocles' *Ajax* 190, *Philoctetes* 417.

[21] Sociability and gaiety before the horror, *The Trojan Women* 511–67; domestic scenes with "I was just doing my hair before the mirror," *Hecuba* 905–52.

[22] *The Trojan Women* 858–59.

penetrated by deception, and are shattered. The ships are to be wrecked on the return.

Athens, too, was the favorite of the gods, and Athens trusted in the impregnability of her walls and the invincibility of her ships. Knavery or stupidity from within can destroy either; or say that the favoring gods desert:

> That mortal who sacks fallen cities is a fool,
> who gives the temples and the tombs, the hallowed places
> of the dead to desolation. His own turn must come.[23]

In the spring of 415, after *The Trojan Women* had been presented, the Athenians embarked on the impossible project of conquering Sicily and making western Greece a part of the Athenian Empire. Their motive feeling, according to Thucydides, was *elpis*, a word which we translate as "hope," but which can stand for the self-deception of easy thinking, the spirit which so often transforms "I want" into "I shall." [24] By the dramatic season of 412, when *Helen* was produced, the invasion had been utterly defeated, two fleets and an army lost, but Athens fought on. The power of Persia was threatening to become a force in Greek affairs again, if the Greeks went on fighting each other; but reconciliation among the Greeks was not unimaginable.

Though certainly affected by such issues, *Helen* is not about them. It is no war drama, but a cheerful, wise, witty —mostly rather slight—little romance [25] of the lost one found. But it also exploits, more clearly than any other

---

[23] *The Trojan Women* 95–97, Poseidon speaking.

[24] See Cornford, *Thucydides Mythistoricus* pp. 167–68.

[25] Perhaps I overrate this play. See Norwood, *Essays on Euripidean Drama*, p. 39, who finds the diction "spongy" and repetitious, and the conspiratorial dialogue between the principals fatally slow. The first essay in this book (pp. 1–51) is the best analysis I know of the faults and virtues of Euripides *as a poet*.

Greek tragedy, a single thematic idea which holds the play together with itself and with its time. This is the theme of illusion. Helen never went to Troy at all. She was (44–45):

> caught up by Hermes, sheathed away
> in films of air

and set down in Egypt. Paris took away a "breathing image" in the likeness of Helen. The Achaeans went to Troy, captured and destroyed it, and out of the ruins, Menelaus secured the phantom wife. On his way home, he was accidentally wrecked on the coast of Egypt. There he and Helen recognized each other and were reunited, as the phantom vanished back into the sky; there they must scheme to escape from the Egyptian King, who has been besieging the faithful wife, and the escape is made through an elaborate tissue of deception; and at the end, Castor and Polydeuces, the starry twins, appear in the sky to halt pursuit, expound their own deification and the future legends of Helen and Menelaus—to brush away all falsehood and let the truth shine.

Illusion is a part of all drama and, most especially, of the story of the lost one found, where the lost one, though dead or far away, stands unrecognized before the one who searches. But I have nowhere found illusion to be so thoroughly the key thought for all action and utterance as in this play. It is on every page of the text. The Messenger, reporting the deception and escape to the king, ends solemnly with his message (1617–18):

> Man's most valuable trait
> is a judicious sense of what not to believe.

All the persons are bewildered with false rumors. Even the eyes can be deceived. Teucer thought he saw Helen at Troy (118–22):

Did you see the poor woman, or have you only heard?

I saw her with my own eyes, as I see you now.

Think. Could this be only an impression, caused by God?

Speak of some other matter, please. No more of her.

You do believe your impression is infallible.

These eyes saw her. When the eyes see, the brain sees too.

The false stories of Helen and the false image of Helen
are played against the virtuous wife which Helen really
was, and she, in turn, against the nature goddess of Sparta.
Behind all appearance there is design (711–13):

> My daughter, the way of God is complex, he is hard
> for us to predict. He moves the pieces and they come
> somehow into a kind of order.

Can we reach it? From thoughts of Troy wrecked for a
false image of Helen, of the Greek fleet wrecked by false
beacons on the return from its false conquest, the Chorus
burst suddenly into the problem (1137–64):

> What is god, what is not god, what is between man
> and god, who shall say? Say he has found
> by thought the way to the ultimate,
> that he has seen god, and come
> back to us, and returned there, and come
> back again, reason's feet leaping
> the void? Who can hope for such success?
> Yourself were born, Helen, daughter to Zeus.
> Winged in the curves of Leda there
> as bird he childed you.
> Yet even you were hallooed through Greece
> as traitress, faithless, rightless, godless. No man's
> thought I can speak of is ever clear.
> The word of god only I found unbroken.

Mindless, all of you, who in the strength of spears
and the tearing edge win your valors
by war, thus stupidly trying
to halt the grief of the world.
For if bloody debate shall settle
the issue, never again
shall hate be gone out of the cities of men.
By hate they won the chambers of Priam's city;
they could have solved by reason and words
the quarrel, Helen, for you.
Now these are given to the Death God below.
On the walls the flame, as of Zeus, lightened and fell.
And you, Helen, on your sorrow bear
more hardships still, and more matter for grieving.

Euripides, a philosophical poet but no philosopher, glances astonishingly at what can only be Socratic dialectic,[26] and glances off again, to Helen, daughter of Leda and the Swan. He glances, with a surer conclusion, to the world around him. Nobody won the Trojan War; and nobody will win the Peloponnesian War: both sides can only lose.

But here, too, he has returned to the tale of Troy before the stasimon is over. The tangle of issues underlying the play, *Helen*, has not distorted its form. But the illusion of the world is the illusion which constructs it, and which is its overtone, or overtheme, and thus its poetry.

[26] This, of course, will be denied by those peculiar people, who seem to be so numerous, who refuse to believe that Socrates ever said or thought any of the important things which Plato represents him as saying and thinking.

VI

EURIPIDES

The Bacchae

EURIPIDES died in Macedonia in 407 or 406 B.C. Three tragedies were brought to Athens after his death and presented by his son, Euripides the younger: they were *Alcmeon in Corinth* (which is lost), *Iphigenia at Aulis*, and *The Bacchae*.[1] The presumption is that these plays were written in Macedonia, but it does not follow that they were aimed exclusively at a Macedonian audience. By this time Euripides knew that he might find readers, if not a presentation, anywhere in the Greek-speaking world.

The story of *The Bacchae* is the story of Dionysus or Bacchus, his return to Thebes, which was his home, and his acknowledgment and acceptance there as a god. Semele, daughter of Cadmus and princess of Thebes, loved by Zeus, conceived Dionysus. Jealous Hera caused her to be blasted before she gave birth, but Zeus put the premature

[1] See Dodds, Introduction to *Euripides: Bacchae*, pp. xxxv–xxxvii.

126

baby into his own belly and fastened him there with golden pins, until it was time for his second birth. Born in Asia, Dionysus returned to Thebes, attended by his company or *thiasos* of Maenads, Bacchae, female worshipers. There he found that his own people did not believe in the divine Dionysus, the son of Zeus and Semele. Semele's sisters, Agave, Ino, and Autonoë, declared that Semele had disgraced herself with some man, had put the blame on Zeus, and had been blasted by him for her lies. Not accepting Dionysus, they naturally would not accept the properties and ceremonies of his worship: the thyrsus (*thyrsos*) or wand, the fawn skin, the sacred cries and words and dances. Dionysus visited them and all the women of Thebes with a frenzy which made them forcibly into Maenads or Bacchae and which drove them out into the forests of Cithaeron. Cadmus, now old, had entrusted Thebes to his grandson, Pentheus, the son of Agave and Echion of the dragon's seed. Pentheus tried to restore order despite the warnings of Cadmus and Tiresias, who accepted Dionysus. He imprisoned the Bacchae whom he caught and arrested, and bound Dionysus himself. The god was in human form and neither Pentheus nor, it seems, the Bacchae themselves, thought of him as anything but a prophet or Baccheus or Bacchic man. Dionysus easily set himself and his followers free, by destroying the palace.

Pentheus now proposed to lead an expedition to the mountains and subdue the wild Maenads, who had routed the villagers and were terrorizing the countryside. Dionysus persuaded him instead to disguise himself as a Maenad and go to spy upon the women, guaranteeing and leading him to believe that he could watch them without being seen. Dionysus seated Pentheus in a tall fir tree, then betrayed him to the Maenads, who tore him to pieces. Agave returned to Thebes bearing her son's head, which she thought was that of a lion, spiked on a thyrsus. In the presence of Cadmus, she came to her senses; Dionysus appeared as manifest god, to explain his anger and his acts, and to direct the weird migration of Cadmus; and, at the end of the tragedy, the grieving father and daughter prepared to go their separate ways from Thebes, forever.

The Bacchae, as it stands, is unique in Euripidean, in Greek, and in all tragedy; but the effects of uniqueness would be much modified if the whole corpus of tragedy had come down to us, for the story of the return of Dionysus and the resistance and punishment of Pentheus was a play story that was adopted more than once, along with the story of Lycurgus, the Thracian king who similarly resisted Dionysus and was also punished.[2] The foundling story which is plainly discernible in the myth is that modification in which the child is divine, where recognition amounts to acknowledgment of divinity and home-coming is establishment of cult in its proper place. Gods in prologue and gods in epilogue are familiar to students of Euripides; here the same god not only speaks both prologue and epilogue, but appears as an actor on stage: miracles occur within the body of the drama. Slaughter by the mob, a constant threat in extant drama, is here carried out, for once, and reported by Messenger. These essentials are demanded by the story and by the fact that the story is a *hieros logos* or *fabula sacra,* a divine mystery of the type which, in most extant tragedy, is lyrically impressed in a choral ode,[3] or ignored. The exceptional formality of most choral meters and the exceptional wildness of certain others seem also to be due to the given story and its implication with ritual.

The Bacchae remains, despite these and other excep-

<hr/>

[2] For versions and variants, see Dodds, *op. cit.,* pp. xxii–xxxv.

[3] As, for instance, *Helen* 1301–68, *Iphigenia in Tauris* 1234–83; less pure types, *Electra* 699–746, *The Phoenician Women* 638–89.

tional features which we shall note, a Euripidean tragedy comparable to its companion pieces. It is not only a *hieros logos*; the divine mystery combines with and actually grows out of heroic legend. The supernatural and the natural courses of events are so combined as to make one course. Dionysus is seen as a young man: his miracles are seen as if they were sense-perceptions. This is everywhere in the language, for instance, in the placing of Pentheus by Dionysus (1063–74):

> And now I saw the stranger do a marvelous thing.
> Grasping the topmost skyward tip of a tall fir
> he bent, bent, bent it down to the dark ground,
> and curved it, like a bow, or as a cartwheel is inscribed
> by compasses that mark its outer running edge.[4]
> So with his hands the stranger bent this mountain tree
> down to the earth, a thing no mortal man could do,
> then, seating Pentheus in the top of the fir boughs
> let it go backward and upright between his hands,
> but gently, taking care not to shake him off, and now
> the tall fir tree stuck up straight into the tall sky
> holding my master seated on its back.

If we think this passage over we cannot believe it, but we can visualize it (or most of it!). Let us make these, provisionally, the terms in which we read the dramatic action of the play, though we shall not be through until we have seen how the action is enlarged in the choral lyrics. Dramatically, the story is not the story of reason or anti-clericalism against intuition and religion, but of one young man, Pentheus, against another young man, Dionysus, the two being neither pure, abstract types nor yet, again, naturals hacked out of a lump of real life, but something in between: dramatic characters.

Opposition to a god can only amount to anything when

---

[4] I am not sure I know what these two lines mean, nor whether the text is sound.

it comes from a considerable person. Pentheus is in the family. He is also King of Thebes, and we can hardly avoid typing him with some of the traditional features of the tragedy tyrant: although he is a little young for that part, which is sometimes doubled with the heavy father, and although we must as always be careful that our patterns do not dictate our directions. Still, as suits the tragedy tyrant, Pentheus is anti-religious, suspicious, opinionated, jealous, and full of horrid threats, though, like all other tragedy tyrants, he is far more given to threatening than to carrying his threats out. He has the good of the state at heart, like the Sophoclean tyrant, however much he may confuse the state with himself. He wrongly believes that he can lead the militia into the hills and subdue the Maenads by main force, but he does not want bloodshed. That is how Dionysus wins his starting point, by suggesting that Pentheus go, first, to *observe* the Maenads.[5]

In this passage, Dionysus begins his capture of Pentheus by suggesting the Maenad disguise, which will enable him to see without being seen. That is, he tempts him with the idea of the invisible man, with the fullest power imaginable for a man—something that hardly any man could refuse if it were offered—since it would make him, as Glaucon says in the *Republic*, able to act "like a god";[6] or like the most powerful single man in the world, the Great King of Persia, who could be unseen and inaccessible whenever he chose, but whose eyes and ears were everywhere, and of whom all Greek tyrants were imperfect copies. But Euripides develops another aspect of the invisible man. Glaucon notes that he could take any woman he chose; Odysseus in *Ajax* and Gyges in Herodotus were able to witness scenes too private to be watched by any except those whose business

[5] Lines 809–46, and note in particular, 836–38.
[6] Plato *Republic* iii.360c.

they were; Ajax in his insanity, the undressing of Candaules' wife.[7] Like them, Pentheus senses something wrong and dangerous, but he is fascinated too. He believes the Maenads are consorting with male beings, and no Greek would blame him, when he could see from his tableware what maenads are supposed to do in the forest.[8] As a matter of fact, he is wrong; these Bacchae are more Amazonian than amorous. We cannot deny that Dionysus works on an inner weakness in Pentheus, the prurient imagination. He does not quite secure him on that alone; for Pentheus hesitates to assume the costume, not trusting the disguised god, and afraid of making a fool of himself. He will never do it while he is in his right mind, as Dionysus admits.[9] It is only when he actually tries on the bacchic costume that he loses control. The costume itself, once on him, sticks—like Medea's robe on Glauce and Nessus' shirt on Heracles—and will not come off, paralyzing his will with inner sickness. He loses his costume and recovers his full senses only in his last moment of life. In his final appearance Pentheus is hardly a human young king, but a pseudo-maenad, a scapegoat, and also the king who dies for his people.

Thus secular psychology has been combined with magic by Euripides to produce the desired end. Nothing will be more futile than to judge Pentheus as if he were a historical character who behaved well or badly in given circumstances. If we do, of course Pentheus will come out badly. But if we

[7] Plato loc. cit.; Sophocles Ajax 66–117; Herodotus i.8–10. The latter two passages have been connected by Rasch, *Sophocles quid debeat Herodoto*, pp. 64–65.

[8] One need scarcely go further than the illustrations in A. Rapp's article in Roscher's *Lexikon*, ii, cols. 2258–83, s.v. "Mainaden," though these are far milder than some others. In Euripides' play, the male consorts, whether men or satyrs, are specifically absent, as are the drunken revels (lines 686–88).

[9] Lines 851–52.

are to judge Pentheus as a real man, we must look at the situation as a real situation. He returns to Thebes to find the women gone mad and beyond control, terrorizing the countryside, apparently under the influence of an uncanny and too attractive stranger with whom the women are fascinated. The new cult of his supposedly dead cousin obviously can be demoralizing, but is supported by the elder statesman and the bishop of Thebes, who seem to be drunk in daylight and are plainly not acting their age. The other Theban men are absent; we must suppose they are useless; actually, the play has no room for them. But the real thing Pentheus faces is the terror in the hills, and he faces it alone. Only some exceptionally sage hero, of a type as rare in heroic legend as in real life, a seasoned captain with the humanity, tolerance, and understanding of a mature philosopher, could meet this situation if it represented a real situation in real life. Which it does not.[10]

Instead, we have the encounter of two *kouroi* or statuesque young men. They are of an age and might be brothers (they are in fact first cousins), and in their mutual cruelties there seems sometimes to be an odd note of friendliness or familiarity. Otherwise, they present a set of oppositions which the directing poet, the costumer and the mask maker could refine on almost infinitely. The one is an athlete, the other a prophet; the strength of Pentheus is sinewy and tense; Dionysus, whose force is easy and superhuman, could be seen as slightly plump, relaxed, and gently smiling in response to the anxious frown of Pentheus. The familiar set of opposed generalities can also be brought in: Greek, male, rational versus barbarian, female, emotional; plus aristo-

[10] I here take issue with Dodds' eloquent assault on the character of Pentheus; see his Introduction to *Euripides: Bacchae*, pp. xxxix–xl. Dodds does seem to treat Pentheus as if he were a real person, and also to approach the play as if it were primarily a document in the history of religion (p. ix).

cratic versus popular and political versus religious. Primarily, though, the action of the drama opposes the two actors. Dionysus has appeared on a human level, and his opponent can offer violence. Pentheus gives the illusion of having a chance and also a choice, though we can not think of any dramatic alternative. Dionysus has told us in the prologue that he had been rejected by those very ones *who ought least* to have rejected him (it is the rejection of himself, not of what he means or stands for, that rankles). He proceeds to have Pentheus destroyed by those *who ought least* to attack him, his mother and aunts. Thus the punishment of both parties is completed in a single act, in terms reminiscent of Actaeon torn by his own hounds or Hippolytus by his own horses.[11]

At the end, when all the action is done, Dionysus, who appears, exalted, as the god from the machine, is challenged and appealed to by Cadmus (1344–49):

Dionysus, we entreat your mercy. We did wrong.

You learned too late. When you should have learned, you would not see.

The truth. We know it. But you come on us too hard.

But I was born a god, and you have outraged me.

But gods should not give way to temper, as men do.

Zeus, my own father, long since said these things should be.

This is not a straight answer. Cadmus gives him up and talks to Agave, and when once again, and once too often,

---

[11] The ironic τοιγάρ σ᾽ἀγῶνες ἀναμένουσιν οὓς ἐχρῆν (line 964) may be referred back to the soberly indignant ἃς ἥκιστα χρῆν of line 26. Hippolytus' own (female) horses, whom he had cared for, and his own father, should be the last to destroy him (1240–42). Actaeon's (female) hounds were similarly ungrateful (*The Bacchae* 337–40). Note that in a different version these hounds were males; see Bowra, *Greek Lyric Poetry*, p. 96.

Dionysus insists on his grievance, his mortal relatives simply ignore him and converse with each other, leaving the god talking to nobody. The last words of the play before the formulaic close are Agave's (1383–87):

> Let me go away
> where bloody Cithaeron will not see me,
> where I can not see Cithaeron, where nothing
> will make me think of a thyrsus again.
> Other women can now be the Bacchae.

Dionysus is established, but it is all pretty bleak. The wild, wonderful life and miraculous vitality of the Bacchae were only a part of the punishment. Where is the joy in the new religion? It is there, not in the strict action, but in the utterances of the Chorus and the dramatic concept of the Bacchae.

Now, if we ask ourselves who are the Bacchae, we realize that the term applies to two entirely different groups, both of which play important but entirely distinct parts in the tragedy. First, there are the Theban Bacchae, the women of Thebes, the unbelievers in Dionysus, who have been driven forcibly into Maenad madness by the god and are camped in their mountain fastness, who never appear before the audience, except when Agave at the end enters mad and joyful, and then regains her sanity and her sorrow before our eyes. But also, there are the Asian Bacchae, the *thiasos* or throng attendant on Dionysus, his disciples, who form the Chorus of the play, and are articulate in lyrics of great fulness and beauty. It is they, presumably, who give their name to be the name of the tragedy; but it is the other Bacchae whom the play is about.

For it is they, the Theban Bacchae, who live the wild phase of life that Dionysus seems to mean, as the first messenger, a Herdsman from the mountain, reports them (677–94):

> The pasturing herds of cattle had begun to climb
> toward the high ground above the trees, just as the sun
> came out to spread his rays and warm the country. There
> I saw three choral companies of women, one
> led by Autonoë, one by your own mother
> Agave. Ino had the third.
> All lay sleeping, their bodies casually disposed,
> some leaning back against the branches of the firs,
> and some among the leafing oaks, heads on the ground
> relaxed—but soberly, not, as you think they were,
> drunk from the wine bowl, or incited by the flute
> to stray alone in the forest and there hunt for love.
>
> Your mother, when she heard the lowing of our horned
> cattle, sprang upright with a sudden cry, and stood
> among the Bacchae, rousing them to wake and stir,
> and they, shaking the warm sleep from their eyes, came up
> lightly and straight, and decorous beyond belief,
> old women and young women and unmarried girls.

The picture continues at loving length. The women arrange their wild clothing; they suckle wild animals, fawns and wolflings; they strike the ground and the rocks, and water jets forth, or wine, or milk; and honey runs from the thyrsus. The Herdsman, who has leave to speak freely, concludes this picture with a burst of enthusiasm (712–13):

> Oh, if you had been there and seen, you would have hailed
> in joyful worship that same god you now dislike.

But the peaceful scene becomes terrible, and the power to work miracles loses its innocence. One of the herdsmen, a country boy who had been too much in the city, suggested that the gazing men catch Agave and bring her in, to win favor with Pentheus. The Messenger himself grabbed at her as she fled by in the sacred dance. The Bacchae went mad. They charged the herdsmen and routed them, fell on the grazing herds and tore them to bits, cows and fighting bulls indiscriminately, then descended on the villages of the valley, carrying off babies and slaughtering men and women.

Nothing can show more sharply the difference between the Theban Bacchae, and the Asian Bacchae of the Chorus. The supernatural fury of the Thebans has just been described; the Chorus remark (775–77):

> Although I am afraid to be outspoken
> in the presence of the king, yet it shall still be said:
> Dionysus is and was a god. There is no god higher;

thus joining the Herdsman in the function of wise, cautious, and somewhat respectful tragic warner in the face of the angry King.

We recall that the temperate Chorus are Maenads by choice and conviction; the Thebans of the mountains are Maenads against their will and as a punishment. Such are the demands of the action; yet there seems to be some strong effort to show the wonder and beauty of this phase of life which the wicked Bacchae live, as well as the terror of it. Their assault on the herds and the villages is a preview of their ultimate destruction of Pentheus, and the Messenger who describes this scene of horror also preludes it with a scene of tranquillity (1051–57):

> There was a corner in the cliffs, and water ran
> through it, and pines grew close and shaded it.
> There the women
> of the wilds were sitting, their hands busy at happy tasks.
> Some were looping the long tendrils up again
> upon their wands, where they had come unwound, and some,
> glad as fillies set free from the painted chariots,
> chanted to Bacchic melody, antiphonal.

Just before the wild creatures go for Pentheus, there is a sudden hush (1084–85):

The air was quiet, and along the wooded glen
the leaves were quiet, you could hear no cry of beasts.

Of course, throughout the text there is constant counter-play of moods and moments luminous with tranquillity against the brutality and darkness of the dominant action. Yet the Theban Bacchae, who form a definite character or set of characters in the action, also emerge as something more, not as if they were an abnormal group whose spell of Bacchic life is only a punishment, but as an ideal group as well, who play out in action the mysteries of the Diony-siac religion—something the Chorus are precluded from doing because of their dramatic duties, one of which is to be always on stage. It is perhaps with religious as well as artistic and dramatic intent that Euripides has so strongly emphasized one of the aspects of the wild Bacchae—their austerity; for though they are fiercely natural, even brutal and beastly, they are not amorous drunks like some Maenads of popular art, and there are no lovers, neither men nor satyrs, in their story.

The Asian Bacchae, the Chorus, seem also to play a double part. As dramatic characters, they are the *thiasos* of Dionysus who have followed him across half the world to Thebes, although they do not quite seem to realize that their beloved priest or group-leader is Dionysus in person.[12] They support him, and the god, but not as an inspired group of women who exhibit in their acts the power of divinity itself. The drama, with its god-as-man against a man, needs a regular Chorus of human beings, and much of the time the Asian Bacchae are serving as just that; in their spoken lines, iambic and trochaic, they are never any-

[12] This seems particularly clear in the trochaic interchange, lines 604–41.

thing else. It is dramatic sequence that demands the theological paradox, that the true Dionysiac life (if there is any such thing; it is never defined) is lived by the unseen, the unwilling Theban Maenads, and as a punishment—not by the Asian *thiasos*, the tame Maenads. These, bound to their choral part, are choral in character. They have no supernatural vigor. They are convinced, not possessed. They stand up for Dionysus and their Leader against the King, with true human courage, being afraid of the King as a man and respectful of him as a King. And at the end, though they have prayed for and gloated in advance over the destruction of Pentheus, they cannot face Agave and the bloody head and Cadmus without pity, that pity which the Chorus must always feel for tragic catastrophe, and which the Maenads of the mountain feel for nothing whatever.

But this duty of chorus-as-character does not nearly exhaust the uses of the Chorus in *The Bacchae*. The defense of Dionysus against Pentheus is constantly enlarging itself into something more general, where we may think we hear —though we can not always trust our perceptions—the poet talking to himself and, rather desperately, mulling the combinations and contradictions of human reason and something that is more powerful still, but unreasonable: his own version of Aeschylus' old proposition, that "science is weaker than nature is, by far." To such thoughts we are led from what begins as a purely dramatic outbreak over Pentheus' impiety (370–401; 416–33):

> Religion,[13] queen among gods,
> and Religion who upon earth

---

[13] 'Οσία. "Holiness," Dodds. "Purity," Murray. See further, Harrison, *Prolegomena*, pp. 599–600. Certainly some things which are ὅσιος are holy, but both "holiness" and "purity" seem too precise and restricted here. I

pass with your golden wings,
do you hear what Pentheus says,
do you hear his impious
uprising against the Bromius, the
son of Semele, who at the feasting
and the flowers, is the foremost
of the blessed immortals? He is the master
of the revels and the singing
of the laughter and flute music.
It is he dispels our worries
when the wine crushed from the clusters
is served at feasts the gods share,
with the ivy, and the revelry,
the bowl, the fellowship, the sleep
at the end.

For the mouth without restraint,
for the callous disbelief,
the end is unhappiness.
The other life is the life
of serenity and thought.
It is unshaken by tempests.
It sustains homes. For the children
of the sky, far in their ether,
yet can keep watch upon mortals, what they do.
To be wise, but to think
beyond human limits, is not wise.
Life is short. If in our short life
we pursue the far, the great ends,
we shall lose what we could have. Such,
as I think, are the ways of thinking
of the men of evil counsel
and the madmen.

translated at first "Piety," for in *Alcestis* 10, ὅσιος (twice, of man and god)
seems to play on the conjoint meanings of *pius* and *sanctus*. But Piety
is also too limited, nor can I conceive of an abstract goddess Piety being
invoked here. I prefer an invocation of Religion and all she means.

Then by way of a third strophe, pure longing for elsewhere,
escape to Paphos on Cyprus, or Olympus in Pieria, we are
led back into new thoughts (416–33):

> The divinity, the son of Zeus,
> takes pleasure in festivals,
> and loves Peace, the giver of good,
> the goddess who makes children live.
> To rich man and poor alike
> he has given as his own gift
> wine and its harmless pleasure.
> He hates those who despise
> the happy life in the daylight
> and the dear darkness
> with wise mind and heart avoiding
> men of power and ambition.
> What the poor
> and the masses believe and do, so would I
> believe and do also.

The defense of Dionysus here is made principally through
a familiar pattern of hedonism, based on pessimism. If life
is hard, anodyne and the illusion of happiness are good, and
Dionysus, if he is no more than wine and festivity, is that.
The originality lies in the way the vision is slid from the
atmosphere of the aristocratic symposium, full of Pindaric
language and Pindaric gallantry,[14] to end with popular reli-

---

[14] καλλιστεφάνοις εὐφροσύναις (line 376), taken up again in ἐν δαιτὶ θεῶν
and κισσοφόροις δ'ἐν θαλίαις ἀνδράσι (lines 383–85), certainly seem to
mean the symposium of gentlemen which makes many Pindaric occasions.
For εὐφρόσυναι possibly = δαὶς θεῶν, Ol.1.58. μερίμνα, μερίμναι (line 381), a
Pindaric favorite (8 occurrences in Rumpel's Lexicon of Pindar, μερίμναμα
being twice attested) is at Ol.1.108, κισσόφορος(line 384) at Ol.2.27,
ἀμφιβάλλομαι (line 385) is at Ol.1.8. The presence of ἄνδρες at the feast
(line 384, Ol.1.17) does not seem to be strictly necessary either time;
in *The Bacchae* it is even mildly out of place. 'Οσία at the opening then
takes her place with Pindar's abstract goddesses invoked, such as Thia
(*Isth.* 5.1), Hora (*Nem.* 8.1.), Hesychia (*Pyth.* 8.1).

gion and the values of the feelings of the masses, inarticulate though they may be.

Against the familiar escape-theme—forgetfulness of evil, lethe in wine and song and sense-pleasure—a negative good, which has little enough to do with the Maenads of the mountain, is stated a more positive kind of escape, the identification with something bigger than the mind-dominated self. Once again, after Pentheus disguised as a Maenad has been led away, the Chorus move perplexingly from sheer outburst to philosophy, first expressing, then stating and defending, the emotions of Bacchic religion (862–96):

> When shall I ever point my white
> feet in the night long dances
> of the bacchanals, throat flung back
> to the dews and the bright air,
> be like a fawn that plays in the green
> paradise of the sylvan grass?
> She fled away from the watchful men,
> the deer hunt and its terror,
> out and over their careful nets:
> the master, holloing to his hounds
> strains them close on the way she went;
> but she, hard running in stormy speed,
> has leapt the brook, and goes now
> on the far grass, in sweet release,
> among the shadows where no man walks
> and the sweeping leaves of the forest.
>
> What is wisdom? What better
> gift can gods give to men
> than the hand of force held
> over our enemy's head?
> And what is good is dear, always.
>
> It moves slowly, but still it moves
> sure, the strength of heaven. It

straightens out and corrects the men
who are opinionated, and stick
in their way, who will not magnify
the divine, but rage in their own conceit.
By their subtleties these obscure
the patient stride of time. They
hunt for what is taboo. No man
should think and practice as if he stood
above all custom and observance.
It costs so little to believe
in the strength of divine
power, whatever divine power is,
which has been established by long belief
and has been established by nature.

The last speaks for itself; whether also for the poet, or
only for the devotees of Dionysus, I will not say. The tran-
sition piece, to me the most puzzling passage in Euripides,
seems to remember the dramatic context. The inspired
kouros, their Leader, has outwrestled the schooled athlete.
The first part of the stasimon, the escape of the young deer,
shows something else, something rare in Greek, something
for which we find a foreshadowing in *Hippolytus*: a love
for the loneliness of the forest, for its own sake, because it
is lonely, or unspoiled, or meaningless, or for all these
reasons.[15] The Messenger who describes the Maenads in

---

[15] Even here, and elsewhere in Greek, I fail to find what Masefield has
expressed once for all:

The men who don't know to the root
The joy of being swift of foot,
Have never known divine and fresh
The glory of the gift of flesh,
Nor felt the feet exult, nor gone
Along a dim road, on and on,
Knowing again the bursting glows
The mating hare in April knows,
Who tingles to the pads for mirth
At being the swiftest thing on earth.

See J. Masefield, *The Everlasting Mercy* (New York, 1911), p. 4

the mountains can only suggest this feeling; only the
Chorus, Bacchae themselves, can express it, whether they
are speaking for themselves, or for their doubles, the
Theban Bacchae, or for the author.

It is, again, only the Chorus who can describe, directly,
the Bacchic experience itself (135–69):

Joyful is he [16] in the mountains, when
from the running, reveling companies
he flings himself on the ground,
when he wears the sacred fawnskin, when he tracks down
the blood of the slain goat, the raw feast and its delight, when
he rushes into the Phrygian, Lydian mountains, and the Bromius
    is his leader.
Eu-oi!
The ground runs milk, it runs wine, it runs the nectar of bees.
The smoke comes as of incense
from Syria when the Bacchic man
holds up his flaming pine torch
from its holder and waves it,
when he runs, when he dances,
when he stirs on the straggler
with his cries, makes him dance,
when he shakes out his soft hair on the wind, and among
their loud cries his voice is deep:
"Go, Bacchae
go, Bacchae
where Tmolus shows in his pride of gold,
dancing for Dionysus,
dance to the rumble of kettledrums,
crying aloud for joy to the joyful god
in Phrygian speech and clamor,
when the sacred flute is pealing the air for the sacred dance
of those who gather and haunt the mountains, the mountains."
And the Bacchic girl, in delight like a young colt
in the field with her mother runs light-footed and leaps.

[16] See Dodds' note on the line. I rather think myself that "he" is "the
Bacchic man."

In wildly mixed meters which must surely be enacted in dance with a drumming accompaniment, this conclusion leads to the appearance of Tiresias, with his half-ritual opening half-line, "who is in the gates?" And the course of the tragedy, the invasion of Thebes from outside and from inside, has begun.

We have seen how the invasion's course runs: the direct story of the return of Dionysus, his establishment of himself in his home, and his vengeance on the resisters and the mockers who would not let him back in. The story is told independently (it could be claimed) of the essential poetry that outrides and interprets the action. The poetry expresses the whole side of life and the world that is here involved. Such expression is dramatically needed. Above and beyond, the odes are spiky with moral questions. Is there a moral to the play? I shall look at a few lines of the Chorus, coming shortly before the last Messenger and the report of catastrophe, lines whose text and sense are disputed,[17] but whose bearing seems, if I understand it right, to go to the heart of this tragedy (1005–1007):

I have no quarrel with wisdom.
I am happy to track it down. Yet there is something else,
something big, something manifest, that directs life toward good.

Toward good: the exodus of the play will not make that point. Toward good if rightly handled? Or is it only the Chorus speaking, of that "good" which comes so "dear" when your hand forces your enemy's head to the ground?

This, or other moral statements, must remain a part, however essential, of the dramatic story or of the poetry. We can not select one thought and shape the play around

[17] I follow, though I can scarcely defend, Murray's interpretation against that of Dodds' only so far as to be sure that wisdom is not a thing rejected. Wisdom, I take it, is not comprehended through any one piece of wisdom (line 395).

it. What the modern critic has to tell himself over and over
again is that *The Bacchae* is not a treatise on maenadism.
Nor on the cult of Dionysus. It is all the harder to remember this because *The Bacchae* is our chief early document
on these subjects.

We can not tie up any tragedy of Euripides in a parcel
and label it. A *fortiori*, we can not do this to Euripides.
There is a place in the confrontation of Dionysus and
Pentheus where the latter asks about the origin of Diony-
siac religion (481–84):

Is this the first place where you have introduced this god?

No. All the barbarian world dances his ritual dances.

Oh yes. Their ideas are much inferior to Greek ideas.

Better in this case. National customs differ.

With any audience, the gentle barbarian will score over
the sneering Greek. It is familiar to find Euripides speaking
up for one who, in Greek context, must be the weaker or
misunderstood party, the barbarian. But look at the solution in *Iphigenia at Aulis*, written about the same time as
The Bacchae. Iphigenia, in a choral flashback like the
memory image in *Agamemnon*, could be a mute victim
("as in a painted scene"). Iphigenia as heroine of her own
play can not be dragged struggling to death. She chooses
her own sacrifice and makes her own pitiful case for it.
The Trojan War needs her death, and the Trojan War
must proceed. The barbarian ravishers must be punished
and the world made safe for Greek womanhood (like
Helen). So (1400–1401):

It is right and proper for Greeks to rule barbarians, mother, not
for barbarians to rule Greeks. The one is slave, the other free.

And there, it seems, the author of *The Trojan Women* rests
his case.

Conclusion

THE frame of a dramatic action is a powerful thing. So is the shape of a piece of verse which invades a man's writing and forces its way in, though it may say what he did not know he thought, or perhaps what he did not think at all. Anyone who has tried much to write in rhyme will acknowledge that the requirements of rhyme have certain effects which are almost chemical in their nature. While, in our less inspired moments, the requirements may force a fifth- or sixth-best choice into a certain situation, and the rhyme may lead us by the nose,[1] at other times the bare frame of sound will surprise us into saying something more inevitably right and eloquent than anything we could have thought of unaided by such a frame. Greek poets did not bind themselves in rhyme, but, even more drastically, in verse schemes requiring strict repetition. When Pindar had achieved that incredibly potent phrase, *palingkoton damasthen*, to end the first strophe of the second Olympian, he was bound to reproduce, for ensuing strophes, that same solemn arrangement of quantities. And sense must emerge under authority of the shape of the verse.

The tragic poets were not "pure" poets. In addition to the shape of the verse they had the shape of the action to

[1] See J. W. Croker's review of Keats's "Endymion," in *The Quarterly Review* XVIV (1818), 204–208. While the tone of this review is unnecessarily disagreeable, the specific criticism is sound.

constrain and to inspire them. As the verse is finest when the pieces find their places in the whole with a rightness that defies reasonable analysis, the action must, to be dramatically convincing, give an illusion of inevitability—whether this ensues from fate, the gods, nature, or the character of a man. The good poet, dramatist, or dramatic poet is a kind of magician. The good thinker dislikes and distrusts magic. So Socrates' "ancient quarrel between poetry and philosophy" is a real thing, although the opposition can or should generate new thoughts. The thinker, who must attack Homer when *The Iliad* has been forced on him as if it were, for instance, von Clausewitz on war, will tend to see *The Bacchae* as what we have just said it is not: a treatise on religion. He will wish to pin Aeschylus down: are you, Aeschylus, for Eteocles or against him? Sophocles speaks of all men as breathing dolls, and of the gods as punishing evil. The wisest of men and the wisest of gods say Ajax is a bad puppet to be punished; but neither puppets nor the punishment of malefactors is material of tragedy, and Ajax, in choosing the terms of his death, makes nonsense of the wisdom of the wise. Or, he would do so if that wisdom were applied in his death scene—which it is not.

But I do not wish to end these studies with an attack on aesthetic criticism, nor indeed with an attack on anything. I have not been trying primarily to establish any one theory of my own, though it is better to take one shape and wrench all tragedy to fit it than to fall into nihilism. The critic is in the necessity of his trade inclined to be a monist, who tries to find the one key to all the meanings in a complex of art or literature. But my last thought here is the same as my first: there is no one exclusive approach to Athenian tragedy, or even to any one tragic poet, but many, and, always within the definite structure of theatrical form, the inner form is alive and various. To try to recognize and re-enact these forms is to enjoy the closest communication with the subject. We shall not come to one fixed, final conclusion. As Euripides put it, or as I think he did:

I have no quarrel with wisdom.
I am happy to track it down. Yet there is something else,
something big, something manifest, that directs life toward good.

Bibliography

Principal Texts Used:

Aeschylus. ed. and tr. H. W. Smyth. London and New York, 2nd. printing, 1927. Contains fragments.

Euripidis Fabulae. ed. G. Murray. 3 vols. Oxford, 1901–1909.

Sophoclis Fabulae. ed. A. C. Pearson. Oxford, 1923.

The Fragments of Sophocles ed. A. C. Pearson. 3 vols. Cambridge, 1917.

Tragicorum Graecorum Fragmenta. ed. A. Nauck. 2d. ed. Leipzig, 1926.

General Bibliography:

Bowra, C. M. Greek Lyric Poetry. Oxford, 1936.

———. Problems in Greek Poetry. Oxford, 1953.

———. Sophoclean Tragedy. Oxford, 1944.

Carpenter, R. Folk Tale, Fiction, and Saga in the Homeric Epics. Berkeley, 1946.

Cornford, F. M. Thucydides Mythistoricus. London, 1907.

Dale, A. M. Euripides: Alcestis. Oxford, 1954.

Dodds, E. R. Euripides: Bacchae. Oxford, 1944.

———. "Euripides the Irrationalist," Classical Review, XLIII (1929), 97–104.

Grube, G. M. A. The Drama of Euripides. London, 1941.

Harrison, J. E. Prolegomena to the Study of the Greek Religion. Cambridge, 1903.

———. Themis. 2d ed. Cambridge, 1927.

Harsh, P. W. A Handbook of Classical Drama. Stanford, 1944.

Ilberg, J. "Sphinx," in W. H. Roscher, Ausführliches Lexikon der griechischen und römischen Mythologie, IV, cols. 1338–1408.

Jaeger, W. Paideia I. English translation of the second edition by G. Highet. New York, 1945.

Jebb, R. C. Sophocles: The Plays and Fragments. Cambridge, 1885–1902.

Kamerbeek, J. C. The Plays of Sophocles: The Ajax. Leiden, 1953.

Kitto, H. D. F. Form and Meaning in Drama. London, 1956.

———. Greek Tragedy. Anchor edition. New York, 1950.

Körte, A. "Sophron," in Pauly-Wissowa, *Real-Encyclopädie der class-ischen Altertumswissenschaft* (2d ed.), Second Series (R-Z), half-vol. V, cols. 1100–1104.

Kranz, W. *Stasimon*. Berlin, 1933.

Lattimore, R. "Aeschylus on the Defeat of Xerxes," *Classical Studies in Honor of William Abbott Oldfather*. Urbana, 1943.

Lloyd-Jones, H. "Zeus in Aeschylus," *Journal of Hellenic Studies*, LXXVI (1956), 55–67.

Murray, G. "Drama," *Encyclopaedia Britannica* (14th ed.), VII, 581–83.

————. "Excursus on the Ritual Forms Preserved in Greek Tragedy," in Harrison, *Themis*, 340–63.

Norwood, G. *Essays on Euripidean Drama*. Berkeley, 1954.

Page, D. L. *Euripides: Medea*. Oxford, 1938.

Pickard-Cambridge. A. W. *Dithyramb, Tragedy, and Comedy*. Oxford, 1927.

————.*The Dramatic Festivals of Athens*. Oxford, 1953.

Pohlenz, M. *Die griechische Tragödie*. 2d ed. Göttingen, 1954.

Post, L. A. *From Homer to Menander*. Berkeley, 1951.

Preller, L. *Griechische Mythologie*. 4th ed. revised by C. Robert. 2 vols. Berlin, 1894–1926.

Rapp, A. "Mainaden," in W. H. Roscher, *Ausführliches Lexikon der griechischen und römischen Mythologie*, II, cols. 2258–83.

Rasch, J. *Sophocles quid debeat Herodoto in rebus ad fabulas exornandas adhibitis* (Diss. Phil. Jena, Vol. X, pt. 2.) Leipzig, 1913.

Robert, C. *Oidipus*. Berlin, 1915.

Schirmer, W. "Makaria," in W. H. Roscher, *Ausführliches Lexikon der griechischen und römischen Mythologie*, II, col. 2291.

Schmid, W. *Geschichte der griechischen Literatur* (Schmid and O. Stählin, in *Handbuch der Altertumswissenschaft*, division VII, part 1, vols. I–V.) Munich, 1929–48.

Thomson, G. *Aeschylus and Athens*. 2d ed. London, 1946.

————. *Aeschylus, The Prometheus Bound*. Cambridge, 1932.

Waldock, A. J. A. *Sophocles the Dramatist*. Cambridge, 1951.

Webster, T. B. L. *An Introduction to Sophocles*. Oxford, 1936.

Whitman, C. H. *Sophocles*. Cambridge, Massachusetts, 1951.

Wilamowitz-Möllendorff, T. von. *Die dramatische Technik des Sophokles*. (Philologische Untersuchungen, 22.) Berlin, 1917.

Wilamowitz-Möllendorff, U. von. *Euripides: Herakles*. First ed. Berlin, 1889.

Index of Passages

This index contains passages from classical authors which have been quoted, translated, or discussed. Minor citations are not listed. References to works in verse are given by line; to works in prose, generally by book, chapter, or both.

	Line, etc.	Page
AESCHYLUS		
Agamemnon	160–78	51
Persians	12–24	34–35
	29–32	35
	249–55	33
	341	32n
	412–28	33–34
	548–53	35–36
	807–22	37
	1030–38	36
Prometheus Bound	82–87	50
	88–92	54
	103–105	48n
	126–35	46
	201–205	50
	222	48
	259–71	53
	436–53	49
	514	95

	Line, etc.	Page
	514–21	48–49
	915–25	52
	1036–53	51
	1052	48n
	1080–93	52
Seven against Thebes	375–421	41–42
	644–48	43n
Suppliant Maidens	58–67	19–20
	83–103	21–22
	93–95	4
	162–63	20
	168–69	20–21
	180–83	15
	223–26	20
	234–36	16
	250–59	15–16
	277–89	16
	335–42	18
	348–53	19
	365–69	22–23
	370–75	23
	524–601	24–26
	595–99	23
	600–601	23
	605–24	32n
	713–23	15
	994–1005	16–17
	1062–73	26–27

ARISTOPHANES

Frogs	949–50	105
	1348	117n

	Line, etc.	Page
ARISTOTLE		
Poetics	4. 1449A	3n
	24. 1460A	19n
	25. 1460B	66
CARCINUS		
Oedipus	798 Nauck	96
EURIPIDES		
Alcestis	10	139n
	958–59	111n
	962–94	48n
	962–1007	112–113
Andromache	279–92	119
	1070	115
Bacchae	135–69	143
	370–401	138–39
	416–33	140
	481–84	145
	604–41	137n
	677–94	135
	712–13	135
	775–77	136
	809–46	130
	851–52	131
	862–96	141–42
	964	133n
	1005–1007	148
	1051–57	136
	1063–74	129
	1084–85	137
	1383–87	134

	Line, etc.	Page
Children of Heracles	608–29	113
Electra	432–51	119
Hecuba	905–52	121n
Helen	44–45	123
	118–22	123–24
	194–95	116
	213–16	116
	711–13	124
	1137–64	124–25
	1451–86	118
	1617–18	123
Heracles	1157–58	118
Hippolytus	1157–72	114–15
	1290–95	118
Iphigenia at Aulis	1400–1401	145
Medea	98–99	107
	107–108	107
	709–730	107
	823–50	118
Orestes	866–956	32n
	1369–1502	32n
	1426–30	116
Phoenician Women	804–805	86n
Trojan Women	95–97	122
	511–67	121n
	858–59	121
HERODOTUS	i. 59. 1–3	96n
	iii. 80–82	95
	iv. 62	76–77

	Line, etc.	Page
	v. 92 B-5	96n
	vi. 107. 1	96n

HESIOD

Theogony
| | 590 | 47n |
| | 965–1020 | 108n |

Works and Days
| | 287–92 | 97 |

LONGINUS
| | 33.5 | 60–61 |

PINDAR

Pythia 3
| | 45–58 | 47n |

PLATO

Republic
| | ii. 360C | 130 |
| | iv. 432D | 89 |

PLUTARCH

De Profectibus in Virtute
| | 7 | 60–61 |

SOPHOCLES

Ajax
	118–33	64–65
	119–20	79
	221–22	64
	257–80	66
	470–72	65
	609–16	66
	635–40	66
	646–92	69–70
	719–814	32n
	756–80	72–73

	Line, etc.	Page
	815–60	74–75
	866–68	60–61
Antigone	249–77	32n
	407–40	32n
	582–625	102
	900–28	61
	1192–1243	32n
	1278–1316	32n
Fragments	432 Nauck	77n
Oedipus Tyrannus	59–61	84
	219–20	84
	233–51	90
	393–98	92
	412–23	99
	443	92
	449–54	84–85
	463–82	98
	569	87–88
	715–19	86
	719	96n
	785–97	92
	863–910	93–94
	924	32n
	946–47	85
	980–82	96n
	1071	88
	1076–85	99
	1171–74	96n
	1182	88
	1251–79	89–90
	1292	91
	1391–1403	100
	1384–90	90

	Line, etc.	Page
	1449–54	81, 100
	1480–81	90
Philoctetes	1316–35	73
Women of Trachis	749–812	32n
	947–49	61
	1101	57
	1143	88–89